SIXTH EDITION

INFORMATION TECHNOLOGY IN PUBLIC LIBRARIES

Chris Batt
*Director of Leisure Services,
London Borough of Croydon*

Library Association Publishing
London

Published by
Library Association Publishing
7 Ridgmount Street
London WC1E 7AE

Library Association Publishing is wholly owned by The Library Association.

First published 1985 by Public Libraries Group
Second edition 1987
Third edition 1990
Fourth edition published by Library Association Publishing 1992
Fifth edition 1994
This sixth edition 1998

British Library Cataloguing in Publication Data
A catalogue record for this book is available from the British Library

ISBN 1-85604-253-7

Typeset in 12/16 pt Times New Roman and Humanist by Library Association Publishing.
Printed and made in Great Britain by Print in Black, Midsomer Norton, Somerset.

Contents

Introduction

Each time I begin the journey of creation that is the outcome of wringing completed questionnaires from recalcitrant librarians, I feel that it must be the last time. Between 1984 and 1994 it seemed that no sooner had final copy gone off to the publishers than it was time to begin again. Five editions in ten years hints at a two-year cycle.

The data for the last edition was harvested in 1993 and despite a steady stream of researchers who have continued to use those data, with the rapid changes that we face edition five now no longer reflects present IT usage in public libraries. Hence edition six! I guess I thought that the last one would be just that, the last. Work intrudes more as does the grey hair that for some strange reasons seems to make time pass more quickly while I move more slowly. Previous editions got done late at night and on Sundays – as the grey encroaches I seem to feel less motivation to stay awake!

The gap since the last edition has, of course, been four years on this occasion. Partly the product of other priorities and partly recognition that things were changing so fast any data would be dead in the water before it hit the news-stands. It should have seemed a longer break – sadly it does not! I cannot imagine why! Since starting the survey last summer I have got a new job, but for some reason Croydon failed to take the old one away. The day job, as they say, has been getting in the way. It has not made me very popular with the publisher and I must thank them here for their patience and forbearing.

Life can play strange tricks at times. I actually began the process of writing up the 1997 survey by drafting some paragraphs for this Introduction – a way of warming up to the task without actually having to face the mountain of data. I started with the following words: 'As I write this Introduction (October 1997) there is a growing sense that for the first time for a long, long time public libraries are achieving some recognition amongst the people that matter.'

Having drafted a few paragraphs I set them aside feeling I could attack the main task. As usual, therefore, the Introduction is one of the last bits to get written. In putting down those words last Autumn, I was trying to reflect the excitement of the *New library: the people's network* report and the enthusiastic noises being made along some of the corridors of power. The strange thing is that my return to the Introduction has coincided, genuinely by chance, with two significant events – one local, the other of national relevance. The latter first: just 45 minutes ago the Department of Culture, Media and Sport put up on their Website the Government's response to the *New library: the people's network* report. I am not going to address the contents since I have yet to read and digest it, but I sense that we can continue to remain encouraged by the Government's attitude to libraries in the initial promise of money, particularly for networked content building.

The second event ties in with the first. A few hours ago Tony Blair launched the Number 10 Website in Croydon Central Library and spent time touring the building and talking to library users. While I am well aware he is trained from long years of experience to sound enthusiastic about everything, he was well briefed about the plans to support public library networking and convinced me that he placed the public library service at the heart of the Information Society revolution. I do not want to overstate these points since some readers may come to this edition months if not years after the event and find it all laughable, or indeed, remember it as an historic moment. Who knows? Nevertheless, to me there is some significance in the sustained interested that there has been in the public library service.

To turn to a practical question, what will the reader find in the pages and chapters that follow? In places it will be 'more of the same', steady growth in the use of information technology both in service provision and the support of administrative and operational routines. Where there is clearly a continuing trend I have made the comparison with previous data and moved on. Where there are new developments I have tried to use what other sources are available to support any projections that I am making. This is particularly true with the development of Internet services where the pace of change means that the data included here are no more than a snapshot of the landscape in mid-1997. Drawing too many conclusions from these data may be dangerous, but it remains important that we continue to review what we are doing and what policies we have for provision of the Internet, precisely because of the close links between Internet access and the emerging 'People's Network'.

I am not going to give anything away at this stage by way of summary of what follows since it would spoil the plot, such as at is. All of the current technologies have been addressed and where possible questions were asked which would allow easy comparison with past surveys. Not possible with the Internet, and in some other areas it has been necessary to change the emphasis. The use of microcomputers for administration used to be a big issue. Today every office is doing it and while doing it effectively is crucial, it is not a matter to concern us here. Online searching as a separate medium is also fast being overtaken by database access through the Internet, with resulting changes in the costs and accessibility. A future survey will thus continue to look as different from the past as this one does.

The one thing different about this edition, which disappoints just slightly, is the fact that for the first time we have failed to hit 100% response. It is not from lack of effort and indeed one of the reasons why the analysis was started later was the begging necessary to get replies. I know the feeling. I suffer the same questionnaire overload you do and have to confess that Croydon's was one of the last to be returned! A line had to be drawn beyond which effort should go into analysis rather than extortion and bribery and as a result two authorities fell through the net. They are both Scottish and it is possible to work out who they are from the data presented in the Appendices, but I will refrain from mentioning names here. From the responses to my begging phone calls I do not think they would be very worried if I did say who they were, but you never know where you will need a friend. Regardless of my disappointment from missing the magic 100, 99% is still not a bad score.

Those early paragraphs written in October 1997 addressed fundamental questions such as, what is the information society, and what roles should we expect in future from the Library and Information Commission, The Library Association, EARL and The Libraries Programme of the European Commission? There is no doubt that within the space of a year agendas have changed dramatically and for the first time there is the glimmer of a way forward.

However, I am not going to dig deeply into such areas now. The publisher is calling and to do justice to each would require extra chapters and extra effort. And, whatever I wrote in October 1997 or April 1998 would almost certainly be out of date in a few months. These are exciting times with the challenge of real change. I hope you find the time to read what follows and that it helps in our shared journey into the future. Please feel free to contact me if you have any comments or corrections to be made. I thought this time all the data would be on the Web for you to explore and play with. Time has beaten me on that one. However, if the work does start again, you will certainly have the chance to send your data online. I promise (I think).

Finally, thanks should go to Alison Gent and Anneliese Wilson who spent part of their work experience in Croydon Libraries inputting data. Without them it would now be the Millennium. I am extremely grateful to Adie Scott who contributed many useful suggestions on the interpretation of data and to Tony Scott for rescuing me when Access (not the credit card) proved intractable. I must also thank Lesley who put up with my late night sojourns hunched over the PC and who read every word as soon as it was written.

Chris Batt

1

The library management system

These days library management systems don't get talked about very much. Conferences, articles and professional debate look outwards into cyberspace rather than inwards to the systems that frequently act as the nervous system and lifeblood of the library service. That is not quite true. I do hear discussion about the practicalities of implementation and operation, but it is usually couched in terms of 'my bad experience is worse than yours'. There are a number of reasons why most excitement and enthusiasm is focused in areas outside the world of the library management system.

First and most obviously we are in the midst of rapid diffusion of the Internet. Other organizations, public and commercial are beginning to encroach into territory previously ruled by us. We have to be aware of and take part in the changes that that is bringing about. The library management system, like the supermarket stock control system is routine and invisible – only of interest when not working effectively. They are also complicated systems doing a variety of tasks at once – check out, check in, OPAC searching, and so on – in a variety of places. I don't need to go on since most readers will be only too aware of the requirements and the limitations of their particular system. There was a time when conferences did focus on the design and operation of 'the library management system which is to come' and I hope those times will return.

I do not blame the manufacturers of the systems for the lack of a brand new, next generation system every year. They are expensive beasts, which are expected to work day in and day out in a range of different libraries and to perform at speeds that avoid queues building and the consequent complaints. Yes, they do fail from time to time, but we should not underestimate the effort that has gone into making them reliable almost all of the time. Reliability is critical and in complex systems, changing too much at once can lead to unforeseen outcomes! Furthermore, the market is small and can be unpredictable. None of us has enough money to invest all that we want in our library management system and that makes us cautious about taking risk.

All of this is not a plea in mitigation for the state of the library management system market. It is a reminder that we cannot expect to produce 'killer app' versions of these systems without defining some new relationships with the suppliers. I will return to what

I believe will be a key component in a rosy future for public libraries, in Chapter 6. Now to the data from the latest returns.

To provide a degree of continuity between current data and the previous 10 years, I have maintained the functional headings 'circulation', 'catalogue' and 'acquisitions', which have been used in the last five surveys. This is now less easy to justify than previously. Libraries are using systems in more open ways so that OPACs can be searched remotely and requests be placed at a distance. What used to be straightforward transactions of check in and check out are now starting to emerge as customer-driven processes through self-issue and self-return. We need now to be as interested in the interfaces that the system offers to the customers as we have in the past been in whether the circulation system is online 'in real time'. I believe it is premature to dig into these new developments at this stage since in my mind it is too early to see any trends appearing. I am certain that in the future we will see more and more library services using the library management system as the customer interface for a wide range of services and I hope that new systems will be available that will facilitate new forms of openness and public accessibility.

CIRCULATION (Appendices 1.1 and 1.2 contain full details of returns)

In 1993, 137 of the 168 library authorities in the UK used an automated system for the control of circulation of resources in one or more service points. That was 82% of the total number of authorities. As we shall see again and again in this edition, the creation of new unitary authorities makes straight comparisons with previous data sets a little harder to present in a form which is easily interpreted. Table 1.1 shows the data up to 1993 and then presents the results for the increased number of library authorities in 1997.

Table 1.1 *Authorities with automated circulation*

	1983	1985	1987	1989	1991	1993	1997		
Counties (E) (39)	31	33	36	37	38	38	Counties (E)	(35)	35
Counties (W) (8)	2	2	3	4	6	6	Unitaries (W)	(22)	21
London (34)	20	22	24	26	28	29	London	(34)	34
Mets (36)	21	22	23	26	30	33	Mets	(36)	35
Non-Mets (5)	0	0	0	1	1	3	Non-Mets	(0)	
N. Ireland (5)	1	2	2	3	5	5	N. Ireland	(5)	5
Scotland (41)	12	12	13	16	21	23	Scotland	(33)	25
							Unitaries (E)	(26)	26
TOTAL (168)	87	93	101	113	129	137		(191)	181
Percentage	52	56	60	68	77	82			95

This may appear a little overpowering at first glance, but the key messages may be easily drawn from the data. The bottom line of the table, which shows the overall percentage of authorities who have automated circulation in at least one service point, is the best summary of progress. We can see that despite the increase in the number of authorities, the total use of systems has increased from 82% to 95% in a period of four years. We are now just 10 authorities short of 100%. Remember that two Scottish authorities failed to respond to the questionnaire so the actual total penetration of automated circulation may be slightly higher.

We can draw some more conclusions from the table. Outside of Scotland there are only two authorities without automated circulation, one in Wales, and one of the English metropolitans (mets). Scotland, with at least six non-automated library services continues a trend which has been visible for a number years. The data in the table for Scotland show that the level of take-up of automated circulation has consistently been lower than the rest of the UK. Clearly, different priorities have meant that other activities have taken precedence. The difference is now not so significant as it was in 1993: then 56% of authorities used automated circulation, now that has risen to at least 76% (remember two Scottish authorities failed to reply to the questionnaire). I think that this change mirrors what has happened elsewhere in the UK since the last survey. The new authorities that have emerged in England and Wales have with just one exception come into existence with circulation automated.

At first glance that might suggest a bumper year for system suppliers in 1996 as the new authorities geared up for their birth on 1 April 1997. The reality is that despite the disaggregation of some large counties into smaller independent units, there remains sensible cooperation in the sharing of pre-existing library management systems. Small may be beautiful, but bigger can still be useful! It will be interesting to see in the coming years whether a viable market develops within the public library sector for smaller systems, which would fit within the spending power of the new unitaries and whether as a result, they will wish to limit cooperation to the transfer of information rather than reliance on a shared system. Certainly, at present the list of shared systems is quite impressive (see Appendix 1.2).

I have always been concerned not to use the data collected in the survey to produce a ranking for library management systems based on the take up of particular models. We are all well aware of the complicated choices that must be made when choosing a system and it will always be the case that what suits one service may not suit another; just as the needs of a public library service may differ from those of an academic library. Nevertheless I am well aware that there is interest in the pattern of system use across the country and to satisfy that interest, Table 1.2 shows that distribution of system suppliers in 1993 and 1997. Be careful when reviewing these data. They do not reflect just purchasing patterns since 1993. If county *A* split into a smaller county and four unitary authorities in April 1997 and they all decided to share the pre-existing system, what was one system has become five! Also, while Appendix 1.1 shows models of systems where provided by respondents, the table merely shows the number of authorities using a particular supplier. The systems could be ten or more years old. So do not assume that the supplier with the biggest figure is the market leader.

Table 1.2 *Distribution of system suppliers*

	1993	1997
ACCLAIM (Belfast Council)		3
ALS	9	13
BLCMP	15	32
Book Plus		2
Bookshelf	14	8
CLSI*	11	
DS	28	36
DYNIX	15	20
GEAC	16	13
GEAC Plus		9
Genesis		8
Heritage		1
IBM	4	3
In-house	11	15
LIBRIS Catalyst		1
McDonnell Douglas	11	11
Oracle/OLIB	2	4
SIRSI/Unicorn		1
Telepen	1	1

* Shown in 1997 as GEAC PLUS

The only additional comment I am prepared to make about Table 1.2 is the obvious one that there are more suppliers than there were before. Whether that means more 'real' competition than before I do not know.

There is one further point which perhaps should have been made at the beginning of this section. When these surveys started at the beginning of the 1980s using an automated circulation system did not imply that an integrated library management system was being used. In those days many of the systems were little more than data capture devices relying on mainframe support to process transactions, and in such situations any access was likely to be limited to microfilm, fiche or printout. That is no longer true. The integration of functionality is now commonplace and the justification for focusing initially on circulation control is based on two points. First the convenience of making easy comparison between surveys and second because it allows some understanding of the extent to which automated circulation has been adopted within the service points of the authority. An indication by a respondent that they use automated circulation does not tell us whether it is in one or all of the services points.

The questionnaire has regularly asked about the number of service points within an authority that are connected to the automated system in real time and in each edition this has been summarized into a set of data showing the percentage of authorities within each administrative type having more than 50% of their service points connected in real time. Presenting a summary of this data has always been a headache and on this occasion I have decided that the easy option is to do no more that present that national total since the breakdown into authority type is complicated by local government reorganization.

When the last survey was done there were 83 library authorities with over 50% of their service points connected to real time circulation: almost exactly 50% of the 168 total authorities. This time the figure is 118 out of 191 or 62%, which is not unlike the level of increase observed between 1991 and 1993: steady rather than dramatic. There will of course, be a rule of diminishing return in relation to the cost of real time connections to distant libraries when those connections are merely used to carry perhaps small numbers of circulation transactions. The equation will change as more reasons for having dedicated systems connections become important: for example providing public access to the Internet or other online information resources.

There are two more pieces of information on circulation to be gleaned from the survey returns. First of all, the number of library authorities where all service points are connected highlights the extent of networking within the authority and thus, possibly the ease of migration to the information superhighway (is it easier to widen the bandwidth than put in connections for the first time?). In 1993 there were 41 authorities and today the figure has risen to 72. This is well over one-third of all authorities where all service points are connected to a real time computer system. Whether that is good or bad depends on one's point of view. There is certainly more research to be done to establish the upgradeability of those connections and the extent to which other authorities continue to extend their real time circulation networks; for example, what financial models are being applied to make decisions about the value of real time connection? The compact urban authority has the advantage on relative compactness, but why have some rural counties decided to complete their networks while others have not? To encourage further questioning, Table 1.3 below shows the breakdown of those 72 library authorities into the various authority types.

Table 1.3 *Breakdown of 'fully connected' authority types*

1997			
Counties (E)	(35)	10	29%
Unitaries (W)	(22)	5	23%
London	(34)	30	88%
Mets	(36)	13	36%
N Ireland	(5)	1	20%
Scotland	(33)	10	30%
Unitaries (E)	(26)	3	12%
TOTAL		72	

The data show that the majority of the authority categories are clustered between 20% and 30% while in London all but four authorities have real time connections to all service points, however, in the new English unitaries the figure is only one in eight. It would be interesting to know more about the reasons for this wide range. Is there more money in London? Are the distances between libraries shorter? Are the levels of use between libraries more evenly distributed than elsewhere? Such factors may influence decisions. It is, of course, not possible to come to definite conclusions from the data collected in the survey. Given that the metropolitan authorities tend, like London authorities, to be compact compared with rural areas, some of the reasons proposed cannot be leading factors. It will be interesting to revisit these data in several years time to see whether the potential developments of national networking have had an impact on the levels.

Finally within this section the use of automated circulation on mobile libraries can be reported. Respondents report 654 mobile libraries in operation of which 144 or 22% are now using automated circulation. There is no previous data to make comparison with this figure so that it is not possible at this stage to make a judgement about the priority placed on automating mobile library issue systems. However, the figure is presented to serve as datum for next time!

THE CATALOGUE (Appendices 1.3 and 1.4 contain full details of returns)

Nobody seems to talk about catalogues any more. There was a time some years ago when library research was little more than 'pushing out the OPAC envelope'. OKAPI, the experimental OPAC at City University in the 1980s suggested that there would be great changes in the way that OPACs could be accessed and in their effectiveness at finding useful material from the sometimes limited information that the search could provide. In the last two editions of this survey I seem to have found quite a bit to say by way of introduction to the section.

Things have moved on. At least the priorities for service managers and for library research seem to have moved away from the OPAC to focus on more general issues of information management and retrieval in cyberspace. I believe that there are several reasons for this shift of emphasis. The most obvious, of course, is the 'push of the Internet', which has proved a magnet to our energies, swinging attention from routine access to library stock to the potential which lurks in the electronic ether. Today you are more likely to find service managers worrying about how to get their existing OPAC onto the Web than paying attention to the effectiveness of the search engine that drives it.

The big hurdle is the creation of the electronic database which drives the OPAC. Once the catalogue of resources is in machine readable form, and there are effective systems in place to sustain the database, attention (and resources) can be turned to other activities. As we shall see later, most libraries appear to have passed that barrier. Building a better OPAC is no less difficult than steering a conversion programme. OPACs come as part of an integrated packaged of functionality, developed by system suppliers who are likely to be nervous of any suggestion that their system should be modified. Most user groups know how hard it is to get changes implemented – even to get contractual functionality operational! Library management systems are complex animals and changing one part could endanger the other bits. We are bound by what we can buy off the shelf, and who wants to buy something that nobody else has tested in anger? Some OPACs now run with a Windows front end, but the potential for local flexibility is limited. To achieve a new paradigm of control over the style and format of the OPAC will require a radical change in the design philosophy of the library management system, breaking big integrated systems into many parts, united by common protocols. A process of disintegration.

Through the 1970s and 1980s the process of catalogue creation and management was the single most important question. In the beginning was the council mainframe and everyone did it their way. With the emergence of the OPAC driven by a standalone real time minicomputer the days of the local mainframe system with batch processing were numbered. Ten years ago (1987) 39 authorities reported that their cataloguing system was integrated with the circulation system – a sharing of bibliographic and transaction data vital to the operation of the OPAC. Twenty-four of those library services in 1987 reported an operational OPAC, while 51 provided online access for staff to the cataloguing database, either through a library management system or a local mainframe.

In 1997 asking questions about the means of managing the catalogue is an irrelevance. Look at the list of systems used in Appendix 1.3 and you will see that the days of the homegrown system are gone. People are buying and using 'off-the-shelf' systems that have an OPAC module: all that is necessary is to 'add the data'!

So on this occasion we can avoid all the discussion about means of production and move right on to the interesting stuff. Table 1.4 shows the data on catalogue availability – how access is provided to customers and to staff – compared with the five previous surveys.

Table 1.4 *Catalogue availability*

	1985	1987	1989	1991	1993	1997
OPAC	7	24	38	56	83	*143
Online to staff only	45	51	66	71	57	40
Fiche/film	68	85	84	85	75	46
Hardcopy	17	23	25	31	30	16

* Includes seven CD-ROM or standalone PC-based OPACs

I must say that I quite like these data. What is appealing to me is the fact that they show a whole lifecycle of development within the public library service. Those people who say that nothing changes can eat these numbers. Table 1.4 encompasses a great deal of work and effort. Starting in 1985 we see that fiche/film is the most common choice for public access with only seven OPACs up and running. At the same time a not inconsiderable number of the library services were providing staff access to their bibliographic databases online. The process of opening up online access started in many places with staff being able to access and process the records in real time.

Looking along the lines of data we see that hardcopy has never done more than offer an interim solution. Expensive and cumbersome printed output never had the same popularity as microform (fiche and film). Between 1987 and 1991 microform was the dominant medium and remains even now the accepted alternative to the OPAC. The row for the OPAC points, of course, to the future. The $64,000 question is not now whether the

OPAC will sustain its dominance, but rather how long it will be before everyone has one? The OPAC is queen. I do not want to overstate the point, but I cannot leave these data without repeating that a rise from seven to 144 OPACs in just 12 years, is a not-inconsiderable shift. It is likely that much of the donkey work of converting data into machine readable form was starting before the figure passed the half century, yet implementing these systems calls for sustained effort and the investment to make online access in libraries possible. Talking of which . . .

The questionnaire sought information on the number of service points connected to the real time network for OPAC access and the number of public terminals provided in those libraries. The survey records 4,094 static service points. Table 1.5 shows the number of service points providing OPAC access and the total number of terminals available both for the current survey and for 1993.

Table 1.5 *Service points with OPAC access and total public terminals*

	1993		1997	
Total service points with OPAC access	842	(21%)	1,939	(48%)
Total public terminals available	1,390		3,366	

The data demonstrate that in the last four years the number of service points providing access to an OPAC has risen from under a quarter (21%) to almost a half (48%). As with the diffusion of real time access to circulation referred to in the previous section, this increase is of no little significance. No judgment can be made here about the quality of the OPAC frontend, the quality of the data or the degree to which the online catalogue is used by library customers, since those questions were not asked. Nevertheless the data show real progress to extending the benefits of OPAC access more widely.

Provision of an OPAC is an important step in the evolution of a public library service. It brings to the customer the opportunity to see not just what might be available, but what is currently available for selection. It brings to the library service the need to understand networking and the transmission of data and is thus a key step towards the networking of non-bibliographic information either through the medium of the OPAC or separately.

ACQUISITIONS (Appendix 1.5 contains full details of returns)

There is nor much to be said about the data in this section. The wide and coordinated use of automated acquisition packages was the last function to be developed. Why was that? Several reasons are significant I suspect. First of all, many library services will not have felt the same pressure to automate the acquisitions process as to automate circulation and catalogue management and delivery. There were long-established systems and it may not have been apparent what economies or benefits might accrue. The second reason is in a sense more practical and direct. Until the advent of EDI and the wide use of

Internet protocol (IP) as a means of data transmission, none of the acquisition packages could claim to be generic such that they could easily handle interaction with a variety of suppliers' servers.

That having been said, as can be seen from Table 1.6, by 1993 there were 111 authorities using automated acquisitions in some form. The majority were using a library management system module, but 29% were using direct links to supplier. Since then the pattern has changed considerably.

Table 1.6 *Automated acquisition*

	1985	1987	1989	1991	1993	1997
Integrated with circulation	11	19	31	52	81	134
Direct link to supplier	7	7	16	12	32	
Inhouse micro	7	3	8	8	7	6
Inhouse mini/mainframe	24	22	28	24	15	5
Other	2	6	2	2	8	
TOTAL	47	50	71	82	111	145

In the past four years the direct link to supplier category has been subsumed into the 'integrated' option, along with the 'other' catchall. The increase to 146 is focused in the 'integrated' category as libraries have found the time and the inclination to develop their integrated modules. At the same time the pressure has been on suppliers to provide improved service at minimum overhead. The result is the increase shown in the table.

The only other fact of interest associated with automated acquisitions is the number of authorities using the EDI standard for the transmission of data. Back in 1993 there were 34 library services who indicated that they were 'actively investigating' EDI. In1997 we have 44 using it as a normal part of their interworking with suppliers. This suggests a maturity of development in the area of acquisitions since protocols such as EDI make platform independence a possibility and thus allow libraries to interwork with a range of suppliers without the need for different procedures, forms, etc. for each of those suppliers. In the previous edition's section on acquisitions I concluded with the following comment, 'There is now more continuity in the pattern of development, but the real "giant leap" will come once people move to EDI and the means of communicating with a range of suppliers becomes a viable and an economic proposition. I do not think it will be long in coming.' That was four years ago. I believe we are now in the position that the comment suggests. The Internet, with its universal protocol has opened opportunities we could not have imagined even a few years ago. But more of that in the next chapter.

CONCLUSIONS

After each of the previous five Chapter 1s has been drafted I have breathed a heavier sigh of relief. Ditto this time! There is always a lot of number crunching in this chapter and doing it first gets it out of the way, but it also quickly becomes a struggle to develop a routine of working which does not descend into a series of disjointed paragraphs, hanging from data tables. The other fact which should not be forgotten is that when work began on the surveys in 1985 housekeeping routines took up all of our time as we struggled with batch processing and/or handknitted software. Those days are gone and we see in the current data clear trends for the future. Standalone library management systems are the way forward, with circulation, catalogue and acquisitions integrated around common databases. The majority of libraries use those systems now, just as the majority of libraries have OPACs and (almost) a majority of service points have access to those OPACs and an equal number of library systems are using automated acquisition.

Through all of this change the services delivered by the library may not have changed one jot. The effectiveness and efficiency of the service should have changed (for the better) but the outputs to the user need not have altered. That is not stated in any pejorative sense – it is simply a statement of fact. The operations described in this chapter are at the heart of the library service, but they are a means to an end rather than the end itself.

What can we expect to see over the next few years? More of the same is the obvious answer. More libraries providing OPACs on more terminals; more libraries using automated acquisitions. That should mean my stress levels will be less since there should not be so much analysis to do and the emergent trends will be self-evident. It is certainly the case that new developments will need watching, recording and reporting. Self-issue remains in its infancy in this country but libraries are beginning to experiment, and more will wish to examine whether self-issue can reduce operational overheads and work reliably during the next few years. The style of the OPAC, the front end, will also be something to examine in detail. This will include the ease of use, the interface, and the performance of the search engine. Within this category it will be interesting to monitor libraries' efforts to ensure that all their customers have full access to their bibliographic database, including people with visual and other disabilities; and those who would prefer to search the catalogue from the comfort of their own home across the Internet, making reservations remotely as they go along. Those are the things that I think will need closer attention in future studies.

2

Librarians in cyberspace: electronic information services

The applications reviewed in this chapter represent the engine room for the development of innovative services in public libraries. Not all of them are very new. Online access to information, for example has been around for 25 years and has been used in public libraries for as long as these surveys have been produced. We must be cautious therefore, not to assume that public librarians are new to the community of cyberspace. They may have arrived in the land of the Internet later than some other professional cousins, but they were using online searching and PCs before the concept of cyberspace was defined.

A variety of technologies are being used to deliver information to library customers. The Internet is a significant force for development, but it is not the only one. We will see convergence on Internet protocols as a means of improving connectivity between different systems, but CD-ROM, for example as a standalone, high capacity cheap medium is likely to stay on the scene for a long time. It is with CD-ROM that this chapter starts.

CD-ROM (Appendices 2.1 and 2.2 contain full details of returns)

If there was ever a new application of IT which swept the public library board it was, and is CD-ROM. It really only started to feature in our consciousness in the last quarter of the 1980s yet no sooner had it appeared than it was being snapped up by libraries left, right and centre. Why? Because of *Bookbank*. CD-ROM delivery of information appeared when we were all becoming prepared for change and it was a technology easy to acquire and use. No tricky connections to the outside world through unreliable modems. You just had to buy a CD drive, plug it into your PC and off you went.

There was and remains something tactile about the CD-ROM which is lacking in many of the new technologies that we use. The CD-ROM occupies real space and can be held, can be played and can be used as a beer mat. Try that with cyberspace. That has been an important fact in the popularization of mass storage in electronic media. For us who were used to buying books, you could buy a CD-ROM, put it in your pocket and carry it home. It seemed somehow easier to deal with the magic of a piece of plastic that could hold 200,000 pages of data and would provide instant access to it! Table 2.1 shows the development of this little wonder since 1989.

Table 2.1 *Use of CD-ROM*

		1989	1991	1993	1997		
Counties (E)	(39)	21	30	34	Counties (E)	(35)	35
Counties (W)	(8)	3	6	7	Unitaries (W)	(22)	21
London	(34)	7	20	26	London	(34)	33
Mets	(36)	10	25	33	Mets	(36)	36
Non-Mets	(5)	0	1	2	Non-Mets	(0)	
N. Ireland	(5)	3	5	4	N. Ireland	(5)	5
Scotland	(41)	5	14	22	Scotland	(33)	30
					Unitaries (E)	(26)	24
TOTAL	(168)	49	101	128		(191)	184
Percentage		29	60	76			96

How much can one say about these data? There are only eight library authorities not reporting the use of CD-ROM in any form: three in Scotland (two of which were 'no-repliers'), three in the new English unitaries, and one each in Wales and London. Here we have an information technology application being used in almost all the library services in the country. I am confident that we will find no other application is so widely used, or with such rapid diffusion.

It is possible to examine more closely how library services are using CD-ROM and what are the most popular databases in use. First, is CD-ROM used mainly as a support tool for staff or as an electronic information resource available for members of the public to use directly? Table 2.2 shows the changes that have taken place between 1993 and 1997.

Table 2.2 *CD-ROM for staff and public use*

	1993		1997	
CD-ROM for staff use	93	(55%)	168	(88%)
Public use	24	(14%)	164	(85%)

These are dramatic increases over four years. What the table tells us is that there has been a 33% increase in the number of authorities providing access for one or more members of staff and a 71% increase in public access. There must be both a caveat and an explanation attached to these figures. The caveat is that the 85% public access does not mean 85% of the population have access to CD-ROM in libraries, or even that 85% of service points provide access. It means only that 85% of the 191 UK library authorities have CD-ROM somewhere, in one or more libraries. That warning is given in no way to detract from the significant shift that there has been in four years, but as a reminder that we should not read into the data things that are not there. The explanation relates to the fact that while the total number of authorities with CD-ROM is 96% only 85% and 88% fall into each of the two categories in Table 2.2. The answer to that is, of course, that some libraries provide one without the other. I do not imagine those reporting public access without staff access actually prohibit staff use. More likely they do not have CD-ROM databases that support the professional activities of the staff: *Bookbank*, etc.

There is information in the survey returns to tell us more about what is happening within individual library services. The questions relating to staff access and public access asked, for the first time, the number of service points with staff or public access so it is possible to assess how widely CD-ROM access has spread. While there is no comparative data from previous surveys we can at least establish the total number of service points where CD-ROM is available. Table 2.3 shows the figures for 1997:

Table 2.3 *Service points with CD-ROM access*

	1997	
Staff only	1016	(25%)
Public	1066	(26%)

So, a quarter of all public library service points in the UK provide public access to CD-ROM databases. It is possible to cut this data in a different way so that a distribution of the percentage of service points with CD-ROM for public access can be shown by authority type (Table 2.4).

Table 2.4 *Service points with CD-ROM by authority type*

		<10%	10–19%	20–9%	30–9%	40–9%	50–9%	60–9%	70–9%	80–9%	>90%
Counties (E)	(35)	12	7	8	2		2		2		2
Unitaries (W)	(22)	3	5	3		2	4		2		1
London	(34)	3	5	1	4	1				3	10
Mets	(36)	10	10	6	3		3	2			2
N Ireland	(5)	2									2
Scotland	(33)	4	8	3	1	3	1	1	1		1
Unitaries (E)	(26)	7	6	1	2	2				1	
	(191)	41	41	22	12	8	10	3	5	4	18

The most obvious fact that we can glean from these data is that most library authorities have CD-ROM for public access in only a minority of their service points. Taking all those below 50% we have 124 authorities out of a total with public access of 164 which is 76% with less than half and further down the scale a quarter of the authorities have public access in fewer than 10% of their libraries. The only region to show any significant variation is London where almost a third of the authorities provide public access to CD-ROM at all of their service points.

Three other questions arising from the data on CD-ROM accessibility can be considered. These are, whether a printing facility is provided alongside public access (the answer is 151 authorities [92%] of the 164 providing public access); whether access is standalone or networked (154 stand alone [94%]). It is understandable that networking CD-ROMs remains a minority activity. It reflects the limited extent of wide area networking between public libraries which can be seen in other applications such as the Internet. Of course, in the future as networks grow there will be economies of scale in 'cloning' disks across networks rather than buying new disks for each site.

Finally, the question 'what databases are the most popular' needs an answer. This last question will take slightly longer to answer than the others. Each respondent was asked to provide details of the ten most popular titles to give some idea of what use is taking place. This is a tricky thing for anyone to do. Assessing customer interest when they may well help themselves is notoriously difficult, and trying to reflect demand over, for example, libraries spread across a county is just as problematic. Nevertheless we have a list of databases that can hint at what is going on. For some libraries this list will be everything they have, for others it may be a small selection. This top ten needs to be looked at with some caution, especially if you happen to be a CD-ROM publisher!

For what it is worth, Table 2.5 shows the 1997 all time top ten CD-ROMs in use in public libraries.

Table 2.5 *Top ten CD-ROMs in public libraries, 1997*

TITLES	
Encarta	66
Guardian	59
Times	56
Bookbank	36
Independent	29
British National Bibliography	29
Financial Times	28
Dorling Kindersley titles	27
UKOP	25
Britannica	21

I must repeat that this table does not represent anything more than an assessment of popularity by one person at a particular moment. It does not suggest that *Bookbank* is not seen as popular by every librarian who uses it, just that some mentioned it and some did not. The same is true of the rest of the titles in the table and all those listed in Appendix 2.2. What can be seen from the list is service managers recognizing there are a number of areas of work where the CD-ROM is a key resource. The information service benefits from newspapers that are instantly accessible just as the electronic encyclopedia provides a new dimension to project work. The business and marketing databases support business information services, while the children's multimedia CD-ROMs are clearly becoming a feature of more and more children's services. Would anyone claim that printed formats are better for any of these activities or indeed for searching for bibliographic sources? I think not.

The last piece of information about the friendly CD-ROM relates to libraries providing loan collections. Ramesis and other suppliers entered the market some time ago with deals whereby they would negotiate licence arrangements with copyright holders so that libraries lending the CD-ROMs could be sure to be free of the risk of prosecution. Not a question asked previously so we cannot make any comparison. In 1997 there were 46 authorities with CD-ROM collections for loan being provided in 244 service points. The distribution of these collections is not even between authorities as can be seen in the data included in Appendix 2.1. A few authorities have larger numbers of collections while the majority have just one or two.

The trends that have been identified in this review of CD-ROM suggest that the medium will continue to be widely used both for staff use and for public access. That cannot be very surprising. The cost of buying into CD-ROM can be low and the benefits significant. Information is more up-to-date, can be presented in innovative ways and will frequently allow the disposal of bulky backfiles. CD-ROM must be the closest to win/win that we can get. Better for us, better for the customers. It has been suggested that CD-ROM is a transient technology and that online access across the Internet will make it unnecessary. In time that may be the case, but I would warn anyone expecting that event to arrive not to hold their breath waiting. CD-ROM rides on the back of a mass market (CD audio) which makes production costs low. Unless something dramatic happens to networking costs in the very near future my advice is buy the CD-ROM and reap the benefits now.

THE INTERNET (Appendices 2.3–2.5 contain full details of returns)

When the last survey was completed in 1994, the Internet did not really fall within the consciousness of the public librarian on the Clapham omnibus, or anywhere else come to that! I well remember in the Autumn of 1993, when I was beavering away to produce copy for the fifth edition being asked by the Joint Information Steering Committee (JISC – the body that oversees IT developments within the academic sector) to lead a project team mandated to establish the value of the Joint Academic Network (JANET – a high bandwidth network connecting all UK universities) to public libraries, and the value of public libraries to JANET.

The study certainly identified a number of important reasons why public libraries should become involved in Internet-based services. However, we also had to point out that with the mushrooming growth of Internet providers during 1993, JANET was not a cheap option and that the Acceptable Use Guidelines (JANET's rules of engagement) for the network prohibited any commercial activity. Hard for public libraries to place a restriction on what is commercial since it would suggest the need to interrogate each customer about why they wanted the information.

At that time no public library to my knowledge had direct access to the Internet. Yet 1993 was probably as close as one can get to a watershed of change without actually falling down the slope on the other side. 1994 would see public libraries beginning to dip their toes in the Internet pool simply by going out and buying accounts with one of the providers at a monthly rate not much more than the average price of a book. 1994 also saw the start of the Croydon Libraries Internet Project (CLIP), a project created to demonstrate the worth of the Internet within public libraries and which served in the event as a valuable demonstrator/testbed for many library service managers exploring the Internet between 1994 and 1996. (The final report of CLIP can be found at **http://www.croydon.gov.uk/index-library.htm**).

All of this is a long-winded way of saying that there are no data from the last edition with which to make any comparison. All is not lost. One of the first projects launched by the Library and Information Commission (in November 1995) was to commission Sarah Ormes, Public Libraries Networking Officer at UKOLN (UK Office of Library and Information Networking), to produce a snapshot of Internet developments in UK public libraries. The resulting report[1] was published soon after Christmas 1996 and was based on responses from all library authorities. The UKOLN survey, therefore, provides the means of assessing change over the 18 months between November 1996 and June 1997. To this end the Internet questions included in the current questionnaire were drafted in liaison with Sarah Ormes at UKOLN to ensure a reasonable basis for comparison.

Let us begin the Internet saga with a simple comparison: the gross number of library authorities who have some form of Internet access, be it one dial-up account, or a high bandwidth leased connections in all libraries (Table 2.6).

Table 2.6 *Percentage of library authorities with Internet access*

	1995	1997
Total UK authorities	53%	77%
England, Wales and Northern Ireland	61%	
Scotland	33%	

Eighteen months of development has moved the total from just over half to just under three-quarters (147 authorities); and that is three-quarters of the new 'bigger-than-ever' total number of authorities. I recall vividly being surprised by the speed of diffusion of CD-ROM technology in 1991. *Bookbank* on CD-ROM. was the incentive: a quantum leap in the quality of information both in timeliness and access routes. The Internet cannot claim to be such a library-centric 'killer app'. The cause of this growth is more to do with experiment and hope than with direct tangible visible benefits. That is not to suggest in any way that public libraries should not experiment. It is merely my interpretation of the reality with which we are faced. Financial entry barriers to the Internet have fallen dramatically over the period of review and many library services who started out unclear about what they might get up to are beginning to make valuable use of their connectivity.

I am heartened by this fact. We have traditionally been a cautious profession: protecting services against the pressures to change because we were aware of the stabilizing effect the public library has within the community. This led to an attitude which demanded certainty about the value of change before any change was implemented. Back when such decisions related to whether or not to switch to a new edition of Dewey there was time to assess and wait for others to make fools of themselves. We do not have that freedom now. We have to be part of the great experiment which is the Information Society and that means rolling up sleeves and having a go.

Knowing that a library authority has access to the Internet tells us nothing about the nature of that access – number of access points, public or just staff access, etc. – and nothing about the uses to which the connection is put. Table 2.7 summarizes questions relating to the diffusion of Internet access within library authorities.

Table 2.7 *Diffusion of Internet access*

	1995		1997	
Service points with Internet access	142	(3.0%)	357	(9%)
Service points providing public access	28	(0.7%)	215	(5%)
Number of workstations with Internet access				
– staff only	355		908	
– public use	39		321	

It cannot come as any surprise to see that all of these figures have increased significantly. A threefold increase in the number of library service points with some form of Internet access is reported here, although it must be pointed out that the total number of service points recorded in 1995 is higher than in the data gathered for this current survey (4,216 in 1995 against 4,095 in 1997). Nevertheless this variation makes only a marginal difference to the comparative percentages. One cannot, of course, help but comment that if there is an intention to connect all public library service points to the Internet, there is a long way to go!

That fact is doubly apparent when looking at the data for public access. In total 87 library authorities (46%) report the provision of public access to the Internet, but 5% of the total service points connected means that 95% are not and that library customers in most parts of the country are going to have to travel some distance to get public library-provided access to the information superhighway. The final set of data included in the table show the ratio between public and staff access. The ratio in 1995 was 9:1 while in 1997 it is 3:1. There has thus been some change of emphasis in making public access a higher priority than it was in 1995: again all quite predictable. As library service managers have become more conscious of the value of public access, and as they have shared the experiences of the pioneers so more toes have been put into more water. However, we may get the figure 321 into some kind of scale of reference when compared with the number of terminals proposed as a minimum for access to the Internet contained in *New library: the people's network*,[2] the ground-breaking study by the Library and Information Commission proposing a national network for public libraries. That figure is 40,000, which suggests there is a long journey ahead.

The next set of Internet data relate to the means of connecting the service points to the host Internet service provider (ISP). There are three possibilities: a dedicated leased line between the individual service point and the ISP; a dial-up connection as used by the vast majority of domestic users, and a connection which forms part of a council-managed wide area network – a corporate network or the network used to deliver the library management system. Table 2.8 shows the distribution of these connections in 1997, compared with the 1995 data.

Table 2.8 *Type of network access*

	1995	1997
Dial-up	69	278
Leased line	15	40
Council network	N/A	130

The N/A in 1995 for the council network is simply that it was not one of the possible responses in that questionnaire. A council network could be classified as a leased line since a dedicated connection is needed to make it work. However, there is a subtle distinction between the two that tells us something about the priorities of the libraries concerned. Those who are using a common carrier network, which is available for a number of uses, are taking advantage of a facility which may be managed (and even paid for) corporately. Those using the direct leased connection to the ISP are likely to be making their own decisions about the service provider and the bandwidth that is required. What the figures in Table 2.8 show quite clearly is that the most common form of connection in use in UK public libraries is still the dial-up connection – the solution with the lowest start up costs. That having been said, the growth of the common carrier connection in whatever form is an interesting demonstration that the library service is part of a wider information technology sector and that there is interest in the Internet beyond the walls of the library service.

The two last categories of questions associated with Internet use relate to the categories of staff using connections and the sort of use to which the connections are put. Unlike the UKOLN survey in 1995, where six categories of staff were used, this year (1997) there were just four. Those deleted are 'all staff' and 'bibliographic services' – the former having returned a relatively low percentage in 1995 and the latter now being subsumed into 'technical (IT staff)'. While this makes a direct comparison somewhat harder Table 2.9 shows the pattern that has emerged during the past two years.

Table 2.9 *Staff use of the Internet*

	1995		1997	
All staff	8	(9%)		
Technical (IT) Staff	38	(42%)	78	(54%)
Reference	59	(66%)	123	(84%)
Bibliographic Services	17	(19%)		
Senior Management	32	(36%)	107	(74%)
Other	15	(17%)	60	(42%)

The percentages in these figures may need a little explaining. These were not 'tick-one-only' questions. What the figures tell us in each of the years is the level of use by particular categories of staff. If we take 1997, 78 against 'technical (IT staff)' means of the 147 authorities with Internet access, 78 (or 54%) said that their technical staff used it.

So, in both surveys, we can see that use by reference staff is highest, but whereas in 1995 technical staff were a not-too-distant second, use by senior management is now increasing. I cannot see that this is very surprising. We would expect to see reference staff using the Internet for information whether accessing the Web or using e-mail and discussion lists. Stumpers (**www.cuis.edu/~stumpers/intro.html**), the Internet Public Library (**www.ipl.sils.umich.edu**) and 'Ask A Librarian' (**www.earl.org/ask/index.htm/**), for example all demonstrate the power of the Internet as a means of sharing ideas and information. Much the same applies to those senior managers. E-mail particularly is an everyday part of the pattern of communication for many senior managers in the public as well as the private sector. Hypothesizing about how a future survey might report these questions, it could be expected that over time more authorities will be reporting that all, or a least the vast majority of staff, have access to the Internet for one reason or another. This view is born our by the final set of data in this section which relates to how staff are actually using the Internet.

As with the previous set of data, some minor changes have been made to categories between the two surveys, although it is still valid to make comparisons between the two years. The data in Table 2.10 support broadly the comments that were made above concerning the groups of staff most commonly using the Internet.

Table 2.10 *Types of staff use of the Internet*

	1995		1997	
Reference enquiry work	59	(66%)	128	(87%)
Professional awareness	49	(54%)	102	(69%)
Communication (E-mail)	83	(92%)	107	(73%)
Exploration/experiment	78	(87%)	120	(82%)
Online databases	40	(44%)	65	(44%)
systems support	19	(21%)	33	(23%)
Cataloguing and acquisitions	8	(8%)	13	(9%)
Other	15	(17%)	8	(6%)

What other conclusions can be evinced from these data? First of all, cataloguing and acquisitions were not a highly rated use for the Internet in 1995 and the same is true in 1997. This is not surprising since both activities relate to commercial activity (the sale of cataloguing records or at least their supply as part of some financial exchange or the transfer of order and invoicing information) and Internet trading has yet to find the systems and traders who are prepared to take the risk unless they can command a mass market.

In those areas where free access is just that, we find that more staff are using the Internet for more uses. With almost 90% of authorities connected using access for reference work we can be sure that the Web and list servers must have something to offer. Nine out of ten reference librarians who expressed this preference cannot be wrong! Exploration and professional awareness cover a wide range of activities and we cannot be certain exactly what these explorers are up to. However, it is a mark of the significance of the Web, discussion lists and the like that so many librarians see value in being part of and examining cyberspace.

One slightly surprising figure is the reduction in the number of authorities reporting the use of e-mail. I suspect that this may be the result of misunderstanding rather than a drop in the level of use. It is quite likely that some respondents will have 'implied' e-mail in answers relating to reference use and exploration, and therefore felt it unnecessary to record e-mail separately. If this is the case it suggests that e-mail, like the telephone before it, is becoming invisible. People use it so regularly that they forget they are doing it. From personal experience I know that the only time I ever think about e-mail as a 'thing' or even as a process is when it is not there: when it is not working.

Of all the data gathered for this survey those relating to the Internet will be the most out of date by the time of publication. We should not, therefore, draw too many profound conclusions from the figures themselves. What should be of interest are the trends that can be inferred from the two years of data. They can, at least, give some feel for the priorities being set by service managers. What will become increasingly important is the distinction between having access to the Internet in support of staff duties – e-mail, information searching, general exploration – and giving and managing the Internet as a public resource for the library's communities. In one sense neither is more important than the other since they are intended for different purposes. However, the implications for the future direction and form of libraries are closely linked to the potency of public access, both in the form of simple access to the Web – access to third-party information resources – and access to Internet-based services created and sustained directly by the library service. It is within this universe of activity that 'The People's Network' will reside and will, therefore demand much of our attention.

There is already evidence that UK public library managers recognize the future potential of the Internet as a means of creating and sharing new resources. EARL (Electronic Access to Resources in Libraries [**www.earl.org.uk**]) is a cooperative venture with a paying membership of over 130 UK local authorities. By creating a forum for services to work together new products have been produced. Specialist content not previous widely available has been gathered together and made available through EARL by the voluntary efforts of public libraries across the UK. EARL is a model of what can be achieved by grassroots effort. EARL may need to reinvent itself in the coming years as the creation of network content becomes a more structured and commercial market, but the achievements of the past two years have done much to give public libraries new recognition as community agents at the cutting edge of developments.

Quite what role public libraries will find themselves playing within the electronic networking movement which is emerging from the policies of the present government remains to be seen. They are certainly likely to remain as vital access routes into the world of cyberspace, both by offering the hardware and by providing suitable training. High quality and diverse content will be critical to success and it may well be that public libraries, if not at the heart of the creation process will be closely involved in the assessment and selection of content to match community demand.

ONLINE SEARCHING (Appendix 2.6 contains full details of returns)

About 25 years ago, when I first saw online searching demonstrated, I was totally amazed. That anyonc could call up a computer on the West Coast and ask it questions in real time and get something akin to useful information back. Of course, £1 a minute seemed too much for the purse of public libraries and anyway the information was specialist stuff on high-brow journal articles. Since that time many public libraries have moved into the medium since a range of business and technical databases emerged as relevant to the needs of public library customers. It was still pricey, but useful.

The Internet is changing all that. Online searching remains a skilled activity and can still be expensive. However, there is convergence, and where I would once very occasionally ask for an expensive online search to help my work, now I get desperate if for more than 30 minutes I cannot send or receive e-mails: in case I miss something vital! Having reviewed above the use of the Internet in some detail this section on online searching can be disposed of fairly quickly and may, next time, be redundant. There is every possibility that the move towards a national public library network will bring with it the negotiating powers of JANET, the Joint Academic Network, where deals are struck with database hosts to provide access to the end-users at a flat rate for the year: a form of bulk buying that guarantees the supplier income while reducing the direct costs to the library service.

Online searching was a valuable resource for many, but that number is now falling. Table 2.11 shows the total number of authorities with online searching capability over the last four surveys.

Table 2.11 *Authorities with online searching capabilities*

1989	1991	1993	1997
97	107	107	64

A technology once used by much more than 50% of authorities is now used by just over a third. Online searching is not longer the monopoly source of up-to-date technical and business information it used to be. Today there is a wide range of CD-ROMs which contain information once found only in remote database hosts. Whether that is company information or access to news services there is competition from other media. The Internet is the most obvious challenge to the work of 'dial-up' online searching. For many, of course, the Internet is a dial-up online source, but the diversity of access and the freedom to surf around means that the traditional restrictions of the online searcher – keep it short, the information may need interpretation when printed out – are gone.

Previous surveys have gone into great depth about the type of terminal used to gain access – PC, dumb terminal, via the circulation system, Prestel – and the population of terminals within libraries. None of those questions seemed particularly relevant to our present situation so I avoided asking them. I did seek views on the database hosts used and Appendix 2.6 lists all the databases identified within the returns. I have added up the most frequently cited titles to match against the most popular ones from previous years (Table 2.12).

Table 2.12 *Most frequently cited databases*

	1989	1991	1993	1997
1	BLAISE (70)	DIALOG (69)	DIALOG (65)	PROFILE (19)
2	DIALOG (63)	BLAISE (66)	BLAISE (62)	Blaise (11)
3	IRS Dialtech (58)	Pergamon (52)	Data-Star (50)	Kompass (11)
4	Acompline (52)	Data-Star (46)	PROFILE (35)	DIALOG (10)
5	Data-Star (43)	Acompline (30)	IRS Dlaltech (30)	ICC (9)

If there is any surprise with these data, it is not the databases. BLAISE has been in first or second positions across the period and DIALOG has never fallen below fourth place. No, the important fact is the significant drop in the number of libraries using the services. BLAISE down from 70 users in 1989 to 11 in 1997, DIALOG from 63 to 10. This marks quite clearly the change in strategy there has been within libraries as a result of the CD-ROM database (BNB on CD-ROM competing with BLAISE, for example). There may remain pockets where online continues to be used as a discrete option in years to come, but the vast majority will see the CD-ROM and Internet access as the most cost-effective means of obtaining data from these types of service.

COMMUNITY INFORMATION/EPIs
(Appendices 2.7 and 2.8 contain full details of returns)

Not so long ago the best we could expect was that IT might help in the administration of community information files. Database management systems might be used to remove the drudgery and repetition of manual systems, allowing easy updating. The resulting data sources were frequently printed and photocopied. One of the things that was striking about data on community information over the years was the speed with which authorities changed their strategies. Libraries would jump from one software package to another, or from PC to Teletext and back again.

In 1997, alongside previously used media we have the Internet. We also have the emergence of council-wide electronic public information systems (EPIs) which through terminals in public buildings and unstaffed 'kiosks' are intended to give wide access to community information for up to 24 hours a day. First of all, focusing on the use of automated techniques for the processing of community information, Table 2.13 shows the overall number of authorities between 1985 and 1997.

Table 2.13 *Authorities using automation in support of community information*

1985	1987	1989	1991	1993	1997
36	69	86	97	113	148
21%	41%	51%	54%	67%	79%

Since 1985 there has been a fourfold increase in the number of authorities using automation in support of community information – another non-surprise. The processes of database management and mailmerge have been ideally suited to the world of community information for some years: at least, the sort of community information that fits the traditional model of what libraries used to collect. I mean by this details of clubs, societies and the like, which presented themselves in convenient packages and could be usefully sorted and categorized.

The technologies being used to manage community information systems are an indicator of the trends which are influencing decisions within public library services. Table 2.14 shows the type of IT application used to provide community information.

Table 2.14 *IT applications used to provide community information*

	1985	1987	1989	1991	1993	1997
PC/database management system	13	27	38	38	42	58
Mainframe	6	12	12	13	14	–
Teletext/private viewdata	8	16	16	18	14	23
Library management system	3	8	15	25	30	65
Wordprocessor	1	6	3	2	4	18

Two comments on the latest data must be made. First, the fact that nobody indicated the use of a mainframe to manage their community information may be due in part to the fact that using a mainframe was not one of the question options! However, the fact that nobody made any effort to provide information to clarify equivocal questions does suggest that the mainframe is no longer what it used to be. The other comment relates to the fact that in the past, library authorities have generally stuck to one technology. In the past I have commented that some seem to have changed from one technology quite regularly, but it has usually been one at a time. On this occasion a number report using more than one of the options listed in Table 2.14. This can be explained by the convergence of technologies. The wordprocessor, once a stand alone non-standard piece of equipment is now the same machine that runs the database, the spreadsheet and so on. It is quite feasible to use a wordprocessing package to prepare data for Teletext or the Internet or indeed for input to a library management system database.

Equally, I suspect that PC databases are being used to prepare information for delivery across library management system networks. The divisions between these technologies are no longer as clear as they once were.

The significant rise in the use of the library management system for the delivery of community information reflects the maturity of more systems. In Chapter 1 we saw how more authorities now have completed networks (or at least connections to most of their service points) and using the community information packages which are now included with some library management systems is likely to be an effective way of transmitting up-to-date information to and from a central database.

The data for 1997 can be reformed to see how the various technologies are spread between different authority types. Table 2.15 shows a breakdown of this information (which was not presented in previous editions).

Table 2.15 *Technologies used for community information by authority type*

	Library management system	Teletext	PC	Word-processor
Counties (E)	13	9	14	1
London	15	7	4	2
Mets	11	5	16	8
N. Ireland	0	0	0	0
Scotland	7	0	13	2
Unitaries (E)	10	2	9	3
Unitaries (W)	9	0	2	2

Here we see the library management system as generally the most popular technology, although the Mets and Scotland use more PCs. The absence of any community information in Northern Ireland is puzzling. The message of the table is that the PC and library management system have become the most frequently used solutions to the management of community information across the UK.

The last set of questions relating to community information sought details of how the information is made available to users. Here we have a new category, the Internet. It is separate from the more traditional form of online delivery of community information through the library management system since the Internet provides access points wherever an Internet subscription is held. The community information is as available to Internet users worldwide as it is to the residents of the particular local authority. That is not the case with online access to the data via the library management system, which is not likely to be available beyond the walls of the library. Providing community information on the Internet can be more than giving access to community resources for that community. It can become a means of economic development and the promotion of tourism precisely because the Web resources can be accessed via a universally accepted protocol. Table 2.16 shows the distribution of formats.

Table 2.16 *Distribution of formats*

	1987	1989	1991	1993	1997
Internet					27
Online for public	26	34	44	45	100
Hardcopy	35	35	31	22	87
Online and hardcopy			10	24	58

There is now more of everything! Direct online access as a means of delivery in some form in some places is now absolutely the norm. The link between hardcopy and online reflects the fact that not all service points may be connected to a suitable network. Even if they are, the library service will have a demand to make the information readily accessible in other locations which may not have network access, e.g. voluntary sector agencies, other council departments.

The move to Internet technology makes that remote access more feasible as other agencies and individuals with PCs find advantage in gaining access to the Internet. Indeed, it is possible that in some cases the incentive to make that decision has been increased by the provision of a community information Website.

Reference to the Internet brings this review conveniently to the last part of the chapter, which reports details of public library involvement in EPIs. These are usually corporate systems which use Internet or other protocols to provide public access points for council and community information. 'Kiosks' is the generic term for the terminals which may be provided in public buildings (like libraries), in transport interchanges, in shopping centres, in fact anywhere where people may congregate and need information. This topic was not covered in previous surveys since the 'kiosk movement' is relatively new, riding on the wave of hole-in-the-wall banking and other self-service resources.

The 1997 returns show 46 library authorities with involvement in EPI systems, of which 25 are using the Internet and have dedicated Websites (URLs provided in Appendix 2.8). In total these systems are provided through 708 terminals that may or may not be dedicated to the EPI. It is likely that some respondents failed to refer to the Internet as a delivery format merely because there are few alternatives!. Within the confines of this survey it has not been possible to dig deeper into this newer area of development. It would be most interesting to know more about where the 535 non-public library terminals are housed, how well they are used and how robust they are. It would be equally interesting to know the role of the public library – manager of the system, partner or simply another outlet. This might tell us something about the status of the library service within the wider authority.

Given potential developments surrounding the People's Network and the National Grid for Learning the management and exploitation of EPIs will become more centre stage. While those networks are focused on particular sectors – libraries and schools – at least to begin with, there will at some stage be a need to make the resources to which the networks give access, available almost literally on every street corner. We know that information is not a product which is easily containable, or which is only needed on special occasions. It is the lifeblood of society and the networking horizons that are becoming visible offer a real chance to make a difference to the lives of everyone. Public librarians are already making an impact in cyberspace and the data in this chapter show that more are 'joining in' all the time. These technologies now represent some of the most potent catalysts for change that the public library service has faced in its 150 year history.

REFERENCES

1 Ormes, S., and Dempsey, L. *Library and Information Commission public library Internet survey*, UKOLN, University of Bath, 1997.

2 *New library: the people's network*, Library and Information Commission, 1997.

3

The public library as IT learning resource

Open learning, or the more politically correct term – lifelong learning, is nothing new in public libraries. The very foundation of the public library movement emerged from the Victorian values of self-help and improvement which were originally enshrined in the Mechanics Institutes. The early public library was a place where people unable to gain an education and betterment through other institutions could enter the world of knowledge and learning on equal terms with everyone else. At least that was the theory.

Through most of this century public libraries have not found themselves at the heart of social change or even very often on the agendas of those people who control or influence the future direction of society. Lifelong learning was not a song being sung widely, yet people have never stopped using public libraries as the means of getting on, of fulfilling themselves.

Today that unacknowledged role has suddenly moved centre stage – cometh the hour, cometh the public library! Lifelong learning is a vital element of the present government agenda as a means of creating a more informed and more adaptable workforce and citizens who have the opportunity to learn about whatever they want. Both the University for Industry and the National Grid for Learning are based on the premise that much of the learning will be done away from traditional institutions of education. Nevertheless a great deal of confusion remains about the nature of lifelong learning and the roles that the public library service will be able to play in the future.

What has drawn this discussion into a survey on the use of IT in public libraries is the trend, first investigated in 1989, of public libraries providing access to microcomputers for their customers. This trend was quickly followed by the government-funded Open for Learning scheme with grants available to public libraries willing to support reskilling through computer assisted learning. Public libraries first started to provide computers for public use early in the 1980s when Bedfordshire Libraries landed a large government grant to provide public access computers and a range of software for community use. Across the 1980s this pioneering project was followed by public libraries first experimenting with BBC micros and other machines for use by children – ComputerTown clubs were popular at the time, bringing children into the library with the opportunity to learn computer skills.

By the end of the 1980s public libraries were beginning to migrate into PCs for hire by adult users. Still there were many other machines in use – Amigas, BBCs, Amstrads and so on, but the march of the PC had begun. By 1993 the majority of machines were PCs and today it would be pointless even to ask such a question. The context in which these developments emerged has also changed radically. What started as a means of attracting new users to libraries is acknowledged as a fundamental means of encouraging access to and the diffusions of the benefits of the information society. The world has turned a long way since those early machines were first plugged in by staff in Bedfordshire.

We now find ourselves cited in government reports as key agents in the development of the information society and companies such as Input/Output make a living entering into partnerships with public libraries to provide telecentre-type services, centres which provide much more than PCs for hire. There you can find Internet access, CD-ROM-based resources and perhaps most significant, training opportunities.

Before any reader makes an accusation that such centres only work in libraries above a certain size and the vast majority of public libraries in the UK are lucky if there is a PC for the staff to use, I will agree that many libraries have remained unaffected. Nevertheless we have come a long way in a few short years. Such activity is no longer considered eccentric or even patronizing. It is quite normal and is set to become the norm as national networking and the real impact of the information society become realities.

Turning now to the figures for the provision of public access micros in 1997 (Appendix 3.1), Table 3.1 shows the data compared with surveys in 1989, 1991 and 1993.

Table 3.1 *Public access micros*

		1989	1991	1993	1997		
Counties (E)	(39)	12	11	17	Counties (E)	(35)	29
Counties (W)	(8)	2	2	1	Unitaries (W)	(22)	18
London	(34)	13	15	17	London	(34)	25
Mets	(36)	11	11	16	Mets	(36)	35
Non-Mets	(5)	1	1	0	Non-Mets	(0)	
N Ireland	(5)	2	2	3	N Ireland	(5)	3
Scotland	(41)	16	17	16	Scotland	(33)	23
					Unitaries (E)	(26)	8
TOTAL	(168)	57	59	70		(191)	141
Percentage		34%	35%	42%			73%

As I always say when introducing new datasets, we must be cautious about extracting more conclusions than actually exist within the evidence. These data show a significant increase in the number of library authorities with public access micros between 1993 and 1997. Well under a half has risen to almost three-quarters. The urgency to establish public access machines is, I am quite certain, driven by a recognition of a niche which no other community organization can easily fulfil; the means to learn IT skills and also the means of exploiting those skills if the library offers PCs for hire alongside open learning resources. The Community Development Foundation in their recent study *The net result*[1] say that while there is a clear and certain need for community resource centres which give every citizen equal access to information technology, these centres need not always been located within public libraries.

I guess that is right in the sense that no one should exclude any location within a community as a focus for community life. The Golden Valley Project's development of telecentres in village halls is an example of this. However, there are still no institutions to match the public's library's commitment to open learning. We can measure that commitment in more than just the 140 authorities who provide micros for public access. The survey records the number of service points where machines are provided and the number of machines that are available. (The distinction between open learning and PCs for hire was not made in previous years). Table 3.2 shows these totals categorized by open learning and PCs for hire.

Table 3.2 *Service points with PCs and total PCs*

	1997
Service points with open learning PCs	354
Total open learning PCs	720
Service points with PCs for hire	240
Total PCs for hire	474

These two sets of data are not, of course totally mutually exclusive. There will certainly be service points where both categories are provided, just as it is possible, though less likely, that the same machines will serve two purposes. The figures for service point penetration tell us that almost 9% of libraries have open learning resources while 6% have PCs for hire (using the base figure of 4,095 services points). Interestingly, the average number of machines within those service points is two in each case. Interesting certainly if you love the random coincidence of numbers, but whether there is any meaning that may be read into such sets of figures is another matter. For sure there are libraries with larger numbers (Croydon and Huyton are two I have seen recently) which suggests that the norm may be one machine in each case!

It is reasonable to ask whether this degree of provision is good or bad. Given the context of emerging government policy which will place emphasis on public access to IT resources and which already is moving the public library services centre stage, should we be more comprehensively committed? One argument goes that these technological resources are not that expensive for the benefit they can bring, particularly in communities that may be remote from alternative access routes. If one looks at the role of the public library within developing countries such as Portugal it is evident that the range of services is generally wider than those available within UK public libraries. All new libraries tend to have PCs for public use, computer assisted learning resources and, of course, the Internet. Despite our longer tradition we have not embraced that view of the future quite so comprehensively.

There is a counter argument which suggests that we should all wait until someone else provides the money, since we have hardly enough to meet the traditional service needs. What priorities are set must reflect local need, but I cannot imagine that the needs of the people whose libraries do or do not provide public access machines can be that different.

The last question asked under the public access micros banner was whether user training schemes were provided. These are schemes where tutors are available to give guidance to help the users. Forty of the 140 authorities indicated that they did so. I suspect the majority of these will be doing so either in collaboration with an educational institution such as an FE college or with a commercial company such as Input/Output. This information will be examined further when considering public library involvement with telecentres, below. What must be said before turning to that question is that even at the level of 9% penetration there is a considerable body of experience on which to focus future development plans for the extension of these resources as part of some national plan.

The European Union, a great advocate of the information society, has made clear in a number of documents the important role of the public library as agent for change and progress within its community. Its unique position and accessibility provide a springboard to the future. Given that professionally we might well subscribe to that view and given that we read in documents about the National Grid for Learning and the People's Network that the government shares that view, we should be making every effort to highlight the strengths, weakness, opportunities and threats of this new line of development. If our experience in Croydon is anything to go by, while we would all argue that the technology is not the important part, it still has a way of getting in the way. We have one and a half members of staff full time in the central library supporting the systems and the work of those staff does not include the informal coaching of confused customers. That is left to the front line staff. I would certainly like to know how libraries in other parts of the country are dealing with these overheads and how the transition is made from the micro as a means of attracting people to come into the library and the micro as a central feature of the library service – the electronic bookshelf, supporting the resources of cyberspace.

The concept of the telecentre is not that easy to define. At least, the question 'When does simple public access to micros turn into telecentre provision?' will be interpreted differently in different places. As a minimum a telecentre anywhere – public library, cybercafé, in a school – will need a range of micros for public use, useful software, computer assisted learning, CD-ROM and access to the Internet. This model of development within UK public libraries has been pioneered by Input/Output who now have (according to this survey) 21 public libraries installed or heading that way. The real advantage of the Input/Output model of development is that it removes the need for capital investment by the library. Provided that the public library can provide sufficient space with good public access, Input/Output will provide all the hardware and software, and the staff to manage it. They will event pay the library a percentage, a regular income.

The fact that Input/Output are a commercial organization does understandably impose some restrictions on the library's action to direct its own destiny. Input/Output expect a return on their investment and therefore charge directly for their services. Moreover, their again quite reasonable expectation to have sole rights within a library may affect the development of future services. It will be interesting to see how the move to free universal access impacts on these public/private relationships.

None of this is said in any way to detract from the developments that Input/Output have supported or those that other companies have supported in a smaller way around the country. Appendix 3.2 lists all of the authorities who claim to have or be planning telecentres. The appendix shows that there are 59 authorities with telecentres installed and running or planned for the near future. Input/Output are the lead player, but other solutions listed include partnerships with educational institutions, other commercial organisations and a fair sprinkling of libraries who have decided to 'just go for it'. The information contained within the appendix is not very objective since it relies on the descriptive comments of respondents. It does however demonstrate the range of strategies which some public libraries have adopted over the past two years to respond to the growing demand for public access to IT.

Lifelong learning is set to become a major growth industry within public libraries during the coming months and years. There is much discussion about what this means and much misunderstanding. Certainly, the public access micros represent a key element of this movement, but while the technology may be demanding, we will have to have very clear in our minds (and in our development plans) exactly what are our expectations and what are those of our customers. The fact that lifelong learning has become fashionable within the 'mainstream' education sector means that discussion has tended to focus on the remodelling of traditional educational experiences into packages that will be usable and acceptable to whole communities. I have listened to speakers who have spoken highly of the role of the public library as a component in the lifelong learning experience, but within the context of tutoring, assessment, qualification and progression. All things associated with existing learning models.

I have nothing against the public library becoming an extension of the local college, university or adult learning centre. Many already have close alliances with such institutions, bridging the gap between formal education and the needs of citizens who are unable or do not wish to be a part of those education systems. Those links will grow in the future as electronic delivery systems allow a far wider sharing of the resources previously only available through didactic forms of teaching. The fact that further and higher education are looking to extend their opportunities directly into communities must not be lost on public libraries. The National Grid for Learning is not a schools network with twiddly bits: it is a network unifying educational resources for everyone, and the public library must be at the very heart of that. I have been saying for a long time that our future will be very much about building and accommodating partnerships. To turn ourselves into educationalists would be to give up the unique skills we possess, but we can act as the bridge connecting our customers and communities to this new world of lifelong learning, in our libraries, in their homes, everywhere.

However. I always think of 'however' as what musicologists would call a surprise cadence. You think the tune or the argument is ending and suddenly with the 'however' chord we find the story continuing along a new route. Why do I introduce my surprise cadence at this point? Well, I have a concern that there is a real danger of lifelong learning being hijacked by the education sector in a way that detracts from the diversity of learning experiences that public libraries have always hosted. It is all about how lifelong learning is defined.

Vocational and academic-based learning are fine by me. Opening those chances to everyone throughout their lives is an excellent mission, yet it misses something so ubiquitous that it is invisible to most people. Learning is something we do each day of our lives, with or without educational input. We learn where the best bargains are, we find out what plants will grow best in shade, we learn vicariously from other people's experiences about the wonders of the world and human creativity. Many times we (I mean all of us) learn those things from reading as much as from talking or observation. Our libraries have been full of people having lifelong learning events for the past 150 years. Indeed, when self-help was the order of the day public libraries were seen as a substitute for formal learning. People could learn everyday things just as much as they could learn another language. It continues to happen today. People use our libraries to find out how to do simple practical things which it would be hard to find any educational institution teaching. Think of the things you do – find the time of a train, look for some information on a company so you can make a complaint, research a holiday destination. I prefer to call this learning for life, which suggests a process of improvement rather than just a process for the sake of it, which is all that lifelong learning implies to me.

There is an immediate challenge for us to ensure that the lifelong learning experience accommodates learning for life, since that is at the heart of future. Think of it as episode learning: we are faced with a practical need or problem and we must learn how to deal with it. How to get from A to B? How to complain? Where to go on holiday? These are all real questions which with help we could deal with better. How many people know about the wonders of Railtrack's route-planning Website? How many people know the diverse range of resources many libraries have to help them deal with complaints? And so it goes on. The future of learning for life will be about packaging guidance for these everyday experiences.

Take the untrained complainer. The future public libraries will provide a route into the resources – the consumer advice centre Website, the Websites associated with the product, the means to e-mail 'Watchdog'. Then there is guidance on how to find company information on the CD-ROM databases; how to locate co-complainers through discussion lists and bulletin boards; how to use a wordprocessor to type a good letter; then the means to type it and fax it. These are all things that we may take for granted, but for perhaps the majority of the population they need support and guidance to learn how to achieve their end. Once learned it is there for the next time.

Public libraries are better placed than any other institution to define and support the needs of episode learning. We have done it informally for years, now it must form the foundation for the lifelong learning movement if the benefits of the informed, learning society are to touch everyone.

REFERENCE

1 *The net result: social inclusion in the information society. Report of the national working party on social inclusion (INSINC)*, IBM, 1997.

4

The price of information: public library charging policies

It may well be true that money cannot buy you love, but it is certainly the most convenient means of acquiring IT equipment. In the preceding chapters I have avoided reference to charging policies because the task of unravelling the data on use was hard enough and also since charging policies represent a significant debating point at this current juncture in our development. It seemed on that basis alone appropriate to draw together all aspects of charging for IT-based resources into one place.

Charging has, of course, always been a sensitive issue for public library service managers. Free access to information has remained enshrined in statute not merely because librarians thought it a good idea. Sadly we do not have the necessary clout. We saw, following the Aslib review[1] that even a government committed to minimizing directly-provided public good services recognized the fundamental importance of a library service free at point of use. The problem which we have always faced with the changes in service delivery and priority is, where to draw the line in the sand? What should be free and what is it reasonable (or expedient) to charge for. Until now we have not been very good at using macro-economic models of costs and benefits to show how charging does or does not influence the nature of use; in the future I think we may have to.

The implications of the People's Network and the National Grid for Learning place us at a watershed. A piecemeal approach to funding and developing new IT-based services, which is how they have developed until now, will not serve well a national policy designed to establish minimum standards everywhere. The People's Network report describes in some detail the likely costs of installing the infrastructure and developing the network content. It is understandably less definite about the funding models that will be applied to creating the capital and revenue streams that will be necessary. We all make some investment in information technology resources, but shifting to the People's Network universe will require significant expenditure at the local level.

How does charging fit into the equation intended to produce empowered citizens? I do not know and I guess that nobody else does either at present. We may all have views, but the outcome will have to be a funding model which is equitable across the land. Some European countries have already decided that providing public access to IT-based resources is no different to the free right to borrow books and obtain information from the public library and, therefore, provide PCs for hire, Internet access, open learning and the like all free at point of use. Finland, Denmark and Portugal are examples of such countries. However the Network is rolled out, an early task will be to present local authorities with an indication of the funding regimes that will be put in place and most particularly what rights of access every citizen should expect.

The questionnaire sought information on charging in five categories of application – CD-ROM, online searching, public access to PCs, open learning and the Internet. Not all of those authorities providing these services answered all of the questions, either because they did not make any charge, or because they did not feel adequately motivated to do so. What we have, therefore, is a sample of practice around the country which is not necessarily fully representative of what is going on. Nevertheless, we can get some idea of the priorities that are being set. We begin with public access to the Internet.

The wide awake reader will recall that in Chapter 2 it was reported that almost three-quarters (141) of public libraries had a connection to the Internet and that 215 service points had access to the Internet for public access and the more numerate reader would have calculated that these 215 service points were within 86 authorities. In response to the question about charges for access to the Internet, 77 meaningful replies were provided. Table 4.1 below shows a summary of the data that is included in Appendix 4.1.

Table 4.1 *Charges for Internet access*

Free	20
£1 per hour	2
£2 per hour	5
£3 per hour	12
£4 per hour	5
£5 per hour	30
£6 per hour	3

The most popular charge for an hour's use of an Internet terminal is £5, with 22 authorities charging what interestingly is the going rate at most Input/Output centres. The next most common charge is nothing! From a subjective assessment of the distribution of these data it would seem that you are most likely to find Internet access free in London and least likely to find it so in the English counties.

Contained within the data in Appendix 4.1 is also some information about charges for printouts, concessions and the rental charge for an e-mail box. This last activity is set to become more common in public libraries as the demand for e-mail access increases ahead of Internet access in the home. The cost of a printout seems to range from 10p to 30p while of the two authorities providing e-mail services one charges £10 rental a year and the other 50p per message.

There is not a great deal more information to be wrung out of these data. It is heartening that of the 78 authorities to report their charging regime for Internet access, over 20% offer the service free of charge. There are constant pressures on services to do more for less and those services that have managed to sustain Internet access free of charge are to be praised for resisting the obvious opportunity of generating income from what might be considered by some an 'added value' service. The reality is that when the People's Network begins, access to the Internet will quickly be a core service, which should by definition be accessible to all, regardless of ability to pay at point of use.

The next category of charging to be considered is public access PCs. In the last chapter we saw that 140 authorities now provide public access PCs or almost three-quarters of all the library services in the UK. In response to the question about what charges, if any, are made for the use of PCs within their libraries, 86 authorities replied. Table 4.2 shows the range of policies reported.

Table 4.2 *Charges for PC use*

No charge	45
£1 per hour	8
£1.25/£1.50 per hour	3
£2.00 per hour	7
£2.50 per hour	3
£3.00 per hour	3
£3.50 per hour	2
£4.00 per hour	2
£5.00 per hour	3
Variable or unclear	6
Input/Output rates	4

So, over half those who replied made no charge for the use of public access PCs. This is a heartening statistic since it suggests that a significant number of service managers have decided that the right of public access to IT resources is something which should be free at point of use; no different from checking the library OPAC. It is quite possible that the 54 'PC-for-hire' authorities who decided not to reply to the question on charges levy extortionate rates for the use of their machines, but I do not think that will be the case. It is quite reasonable for the service manager to make a judgement that the only means of sustaining the service is to make a charge – we have done that for years with audio material and in some libraries with language courses.

On the other hand the fact that a significant number have decided to provide the service free of charge is a useful indicator for the roll out of The People's Network: at least in as much as it shows that a goodly number of libraries have not felt the need to recoup costs having contained expenditure within their revenue budgets. Table 4.3 shows the authorities where there is no charge distributed between the various authority types and shown as a percentage of the total population of each type. The English metropolitan authorities are clearly well ahead on the number offering free access to PCs, with all of the other authorities some way behind.

Table 4.3 *Libraries with no charge for PC use by authority type*

	Respondents	% no charge
Counties	5	14
London	4	13
Met districts	18	50
Northern Ireland	1	25
Scotland	7	21
Unitaries (England)	4	18
Unitaries (Wales)	6	17

These are only indicators, not objective data, since we only have the information from those who decided to answer the question. The figures suggest that London is not the best place to look for a free PC to use.

At present such information ought to help those beginning to think about the implementation of The People's Network; in the future it will be vital information to ensure that there is a consistent and equitable approach to the provision of these services right across the land.

And so to the CD-ROM for reference use and for loan. This is a fairly simple set of data on which to report (see Appendix 4.3). As one might expect for public access to a resource which frequently acts directly as a substitute for traditional book-based information, there is not a single respondent who indicated a blanket charge for the use of CD-ROM within the library. Indeed only three out the of 132 who replied to this question indicated that they made any direct charge at all, except for printouts. Bromley, Oxfordshire and York libraries make a charge for the use of certain business and market research databases, while York also indicated printout charge only for other databases. That does not mean other libraries do not make a charge for such specialist resources, merely that only Bromley and York replied to the question. While 132 replies were received there are 164 library authorities giving direct public access to CD-ROM databases.

Of all the remaining replies there were only two choices – free access with a charge for printouts (95), or no charge whatsoever (37). Where printout charges are levied they range from 2p to 50p for black and white and up to 50p for colour. The most cited charges are 10p and 20p which I suspect tie in with copying charges in those libraries. There is little more that can be said about these data. It would be extremely surprising to find charges being made to access CD-ROMs within libraries since they are now such an integral part of core service. To make a charge for access to resources which support students and local businesses would act as a barrier and at the same time transfer the demand to traditional and less effective resources. People would expect the printed versions of databases to be available! Twenty-eight respondents also reported on charges for the loan of CD-ROM. The lowest charge is 70p for two weeks, the average around £1.50 per week.

A not dissimilar picture to in-library CD-ROM use emerges from an analysis of the replies to the question on charges for the use of open learning materials. These services started with grant support from government several years ago, and Chapter 3 reported on the number of access points now available for computer assisted learning. The Open for Learning movement started by the intervention of government was focused quite specifically on basic IT skills, providing the means for people to develop their use of computers both by in-library use and lending collections of software, videos and workbooks. The range of options for charging thus include an annual fee, an hourly rate, a rental charge for borrowing, or charging nothing.

Table 4.4 shows that distribution of responses from the 100 replies.

Table 4.4 *Charges for use of open learning materials*

No charge	78
Annual subscription	14
Rental	6
Variable	2

The most common strategy by far is clearly to make no direct charge for the service. Some of those libraries providing the service without subscription or rental do make a charge for printing in similar vein to those charges made for printed reports from CD-ROM. As with public access PCs this level of free access shows a commitment by service managers to make these services as accessible as possible. Those libraries that are making a subscription or rental charge are doing so to support the purchase of new resources for the service and have not, as yet been able to absorb completely the costs within the service's revenue budgets.

One final word on charges for open learning resources must be offered about those authorities making charges. Of the 20 within the categories annual subscription and rental 13 are in London. So as was seen with public access PCs London is not the best place to look for free access. This may be explained in a number of ways. First, of course, the data are not comprehensive – they are merely the results of those people who decided to fill in that particular box. However, if we assume that the sample is not too biased in any one direction, then it may well be London public libraries find themselves a part of a range of opportunities for training and re-skilling which are more densely spread than outside the capital. Cybercafés, training centres, adult education, etc. are not unique to London, but they are perhaps more readily available within easy travelling distance than elsewhere in the country. This is hypothesis and there may be other reasons why London libraries seem more likely to charge for open learning resources which are not obviously apparent.

Finally within the section of the questionnaire on charging comes online searching. This is the IT information service with the longest history in public libraries and in past surveys it has been clear that there are two common factors which have influenced charging policies. The first is making the decision whether to charge at all. In the past many libraries have indicated that should a member of staff decide that an online search is the easiest/most effective way to deal with an enquiry no charge should be made to the user. Where the user asks specifically for an online search, perhaps for company information, this has generally been charged for. The second factor is the level of charge. Online searching was never a cheap undertaking, particularly when there was little choice but to pay BT for dial-up connections. Since online hosts charged per connection and since the overall costs were high, libraries generally followed the 'cost recovery' route of passing on all the direct costs to the user, and frequently adding in the overhead of staff time since the search was (and remains) a skilled activity.

The data for 1997, which are shown in Appendix 4.5, show that nothing much has changed. There are 77 replies and of those, 38 authorities indicate that they continue to follow a full cost-recovery type strategy. I have interpreted the information in Appendix 4.5 quite generously to come to that figure, but it does seem overall that the level of charges indicated reflects an approach designed to recoup the costs involved. In some cases exceptions are shown where the enquiry is from a private individual rather than a commercial organization but that is the exception. There are nine authorities indicating no charges whatsoever for the service, which may mean that the search is always at 'staff discretion'. Whether a positive decision to support local business has been taken or whether there is little demand, or indeed whether the databases provided are of low cost or low value is not known. Yet whatever the reasons for the decision not to make any charge, it remains exceptional within the data shown in the appendix. During the next two years, that situation may change as more online hosts transfer to the Internet and find new markets offering high use and expecting low cost. This will start to impact on the costs which public libraries are currently faced with. The arrival of The People's Network may also change the pattern of use of online hosts.

Within the academic sector the centralized management of the Joint Academic Network (JANET) has enabled bulk discounts to be negotiated for university access to online hosts. It is to be expected that similar deals will be struck for public libraries through the People's Network. This could reduce significantly the costs currently incurred, especially if the access route is via a dedicated connection to the network rather than per minute dial-up costs.

The pattern of charging which has been described in this chapter is not directly comparable with previous surveys, mainly because wide provision of many of the services is relatively recent. While there are few comparators, it is interesting to me how far those libraries who replied to the questions have been able to sustain the services while making no charges for their use. The 20 giving free access to the Internet are outnumbered by the libraries making a charge, but of the total providing public access to the Internet finding 20 prepared to bear the costs directly at this stage of development is good news and an example for others to follow. The same is true for public access PCs and open learning where the majority in both cases make no charge.

We are bound to find more incentive to review our policies in the future as The People's Network begins to affect what we do. We will all need to think very clearly both about what are the new responsibilities we will adopt as the Network becomes the backbone of a national information/lifelong learning policy, and also about how we are to respond financially to those new roles. As I write we do not know what level of external investment in the Network will be made or where the money will come from. The new public access IT services reported in this survey will be but a drop in the ocean if all service points are to be connected to give access to diverse new resources. Someone will have to pay the set up and operational costs of that and, if equality of access is a basic principle funding models which do not rely on direct charging will be necessary. What is reported here is at least a good beginning. Public library managers have generally found the means to avoid charging; let us hope that the promised government intervention allows us to retain and extend that trend.

REFERENCE

1 *A review of the public library service in England and Wales. Final report*, London, Aslib, 1995.

5

Systems management and future plans

The first four chapters have focused on the use and operation of particular technologies and have to a considerable degree been based around quantifiable statistics. They may not have been fully comprehensive, but they were numbers that could be counted. In turning to the management and future planning of those services quantification is not so easy. In recent surveys respondents were asked to make an assessment of progress since the last survey by saying what they had achieved and then what they expected to achieve in the next year. I always hoped this would provide a straightforward means of seeing what had happened and what would happen. It was never very easy to make sense of the results partly because what seemed logical to me was obviously not so for the victims at the other end. Moreover people interpret things within the context of their own circumstances.

The outcome was thus a headache for me and a chapter which could survey the data, but which could not be as deductive as was expected. For those reasons and more I decided this time to simplify the process and just provide a series of free response boxes with the briefest of guidance on what to do. The two questions of importance concern management and training and future plans, and these were expressed as follows:

> Management and training – please describe arrangements for the technical management of systems, e.g. Specialist staff, etc., and any arrangements for staff training and awareness;

> Future plans – please describe any concrete plans for IT developments which you think it will be possible to complete by the end of 1997/98.

Two further questions were added to this section, one to establish the extent to which IT strategies have been developed and the other to provide the opportunity for respondents to provide information which would not fit into any of the other questions.

There is a downside to allowing free expression. People provide considerable information, but the format, content and length vary significantly. The result is a great deal of useful data, but without the framework necessary to produce summary totals within activities, approaches and categories; or at least not without a great deal of analytical effort. All of the data from these questions is included in the Appendices and if anyone is really keen to dig deep then I will happily discuss providing the data on disk. For me, given the demands of time I am going to take a broad brush approach and try to find the most significant nuggets from all of the information that has been provided, and there is a great deal included in the appendices relating to Chapter 5 (Appendices 5.1–5.4).

We will start with the information on management and training. One hundred and sixty-eight authorities chose to write something in the box and what they wrote is fairly diverse! I have had to exercise considerable 'interpreter's licence' to produce some comparisons from this information. Not all respondents reported on management and training and, of course, within these two categories a variety of strategies may be reported within an individual library service. Furthermore, some things which are not reported must be implied. For example, 181 libraries have library management systems, all of which will need some external support for their management. The normal strategy is a maintenance contract with the supplier to support as a minimum the system centre and the software. Library management system software is not something for the inexperienced or the faint hearted! Yet only 27 respondents reported that they received support from their system supplier. We must assume therefore that many of the others did not consider such an obvious relationship worthy of mention.

I have reviewed all of the replies and by counting key words and the general sense of what is reported have produced what I feel is the best attempt at a summary of the data. I will repeat that there is probably more to be done with all the data of this chapter, but it would take some considerable time and in some cases would involve further contact with the authorities themselves to elaborate the replies.

Overall, what seems to emerge from my analysis is a picture of the majority of library services as relatively self-contained for the management and development of their IT systems. Of the 166 who replied 111 said that they manage all or some of their systems themselves, inhouse. This is certainly the case with the management of the library management system where the role of the systems manager seems to be alive and well. The development of other systems such as Internet and CD-ROM for public use is also managed inhouse in many cases. The closest runner up to inhouse as the main means of management is for management, technical support and training to be provided corporately within the local authority, usually by the IT unit. This approach was cited 66 times. I do not find these patterns too surprising. It is not overstating the case to suggest that many public libraries are at the cutting edge of IT developments within their authorities, exploring CD-ROM, Internet and access to public information in ways still to be fully understood by other departments. On the other hand, where the IT unit has broken the shackles of the 'mainframe mentality', there can be useful synergy. My experience is that where libraries are developing new systems, IT unit staff will be interested in the new and the different.

The figures quoted in these categories are no more than trend indicators. The reality is that many of the libraries who are running library management systems and other services across corporate, common carrier networks are part of the council's wider support and management framework. From what I have said above, therefore, the most likely combination of support resources in the majority of places will be an inhouse team developing systems and maintaining the library management system, with some support from the corporate resources and maintenance contracts with relevant system suppliers.

All of the other categories within the management and training box had significantly lower responses. Nine libraries referred to 'ad hoc' or 'various' relationships and nine also indicated that external organizations (such as Input/Output) were involved in staff training. Five reported using facilities management companies to run their library management systems and a further five said that all the arrangements were the subject of current review. One authority reported merely that the Systems Manager post was frozen and another that there were 'no formal arrangements'. Good luck to both of them, I say. Finally, 14 library services reported that their library management systems, and in some cases other IT systems, were operated in partnerships with other library authorities. All of these were new unitaries who have found it essential, at least in the short term, to work with the adjacent county to share the pre-existing system. Several of those new unitaries indicated that they were considering migrating to their own standalone systems.

It is appropriate next to review the role and importance of the IT strategy as a means of guiding developments. The survey asked first 'do you have a written-down IT strategy for your service?' and then, 'if so, please could you enclose a copy?' To the first question, 51 people responded with a 'yes'. To the second 17 authorities provided strategy documents. That is actually not quite correct. Nineteen documents were received, but one of them was a general Council-wide strategy and one was just six bullet points. While neither would fall into the class of library IT strategy documents as detailed in Alec Gallimore's recent study,[1] the latter was at least concise to the point where few could claim not to have the time to read it!

Of the total figure of 51 authorities who have library IT strategies there is not a great deal that can be said. The fact that over a quarter of all library services have such strategic documents and are presumably using them shows a commitment to sustaining and developing these vital services. Perhaps just as interesting is what the other three-quarters do in planning how resources are used most effectively. I do not ask the question with any sense of criticism. I find it very hard to see how a formal planning framework would ever be able to deal with the volatility of IT developments at present, and revising a comprehensive development plan might well become a full time occupation. And I do not say that to offer criticism to those library services who kindly sent me copies of their very comprehensive plans. There is a tight-rope to be walked at present. We must have a vision of what we expect to achieve and we must try to gather the resources that are needed to deliver that vision. The nature of local government suggests on that basis alone we should be operating within a framework which communicates clearly our intentions and the outcomes to colleagues and political masters. As an aside, it is interesting that several of the strategy documents were actually committee reports rather then management documents.

Given the uncertainties we face any plan must be capable of modification in midstream. Decisions by education departments to spend some money, the discovery of a local company looking for some partnership to develop their IT product are all opportunities that should not be ignored, and strategies must be able to accommodate them. On the other hand any library service that does not have some vision of what it is trying to achieve through IT (with or without a plan) is going to find it quite hard to deliver in any meaningful way. So something, a mental model, someone with vision, or a strategic plan is essential. Of the 17 plans received several were, as already mentioned, copies of committee reports. Others were fully worked up development plans with sections defining the present position, the vision, the expected costs, the resources available and precise timescales. Brave people.

In between were a number that presented a general direction for development – the vision plus some proposals for actions. One of the respondents described their strategy as a 'wish list of services' and I think that is probably a fair description of a number of them. It is a good thing to have something like that providing options and ideas which are available when needed, either for the elected member or the sudden windfall.

The last piece of information to be gleaned from the replies about IT strategies concerns the distribution of the authorities who reported having them. Table 5.1 below shows the number from each type of local authority and then shows the figure as a percentage of the total authorities in the category:

Table 5.1 *Distribution of authorities having an IT strategy*

	IT strategies	Percentage of total
Counties (E)	19	54
London	8	24
Met districts	10	25
Northern Ireland	1	19
Scotland	4	20
Unitaries (E)	4	12
Unitaries (W)	5	18

Clearly, if you are an IT strategy freak the English counties are the place for you. The reasons for the larger number in counties? Size perhaps and the wide distribution of services and people – the strategy as a means of passing a message; or a different tradition placing an emphasis on longer term planning not so apparent in other authority types. Maybe it is just an attempt to manage resources that are disappearing faster than elsewhere. I can only guess at the reason.

Turning from the general question about whether or not a planning process was in place respondents were asked to comment on 'concrete plans . . . it will be possible to implement by the end of 1997/98.' Within the 158 replies received there were, not surprisingly, some common themes. Replacing, extending or enhancing the library management system and more usc of thc Internet were head and shoulders above the pack with 82 and 87 mentions respectively with the closest runner up to those two being extending access to CD-ROMs at 47. All three of these are naturally key parts of service development.

Activity associated with the library management system was mainly replacing the existing system or extending the network to additional service points. On top of non-specific indication of changes or enhancements, 14 libraries planned to enhance or extend access to the OPAC and three to start to use an automated acquisitions package. Within the Internet category there were two main intentions – to increase public access or to develop Web content, for example, by managing the Council Website. Seven specifically mentioned managing or contributing to corporate information services on the Web and extracting those seven from the 87 above leaves 80 library services planning to begin or extend public access to the Internet. In similar vein an increase in CD-ROM based services is a continuation of the switch from traditional media where it is evident that there are to be efficiency and effectiveness gains.

Some way behind the three front runners of library management system, CD-ROM and Internet come community information and EPIs with 27, open learning with16, PCs for hire with 15 and EDI with six. Not on the same scale perhaps, but all useful developments to promote. Finally, a number of rogue replies can be drawn together under a catch-all heading. This heading included three libraries who just said that nothing was going on and another that said 'end of current system in December 1997' without any further indication of what action was likely to be taken to remedy this situation! Other low level mentions included, self-issue, IT specifically for youth, IT for the housebound (2), voice recognition, kiosks (2), Input/Output (2), public e-mail (4), and serials management. Finally reference was made by one person to the creation of a virtual museum.

The last 'please fill in' box asked for any final comments. Some of the correspondents were obviously in the swing by this question since they extemporized further on replies that were provided for previous questions. This got 61 answers and the nature of the question – any other comments? – meant that not too many common themes would be seen. Of those 61, 14 did say that they were in the middle of strategy preparation so more versions of such documents will be available next time the survey is done. Seven authorities commented on the need to respond to change although underlining the different perceptions that abound, two cancelled each other out: one by saying that progress was slow, while another stated just the opposite. I suspect that one was commenting on the slow rate of change within the parent organization while the other was reflecting on the problems of trying to keep pace with the fast-changing world outside the organization. Three authorities made reference to the need for library services to define clearly the role of the library within the information society and several made reference to enhancements necessary to improve corporate wide area networks. Five reported the hoped for replacement of the library management system.

Alongside the comments which could be categorized were a number that were 'stand-alone'. Examples include the importance of partnerships with external organizations, the need for a vision, the need for culture shift within the authority, using IT to overcome rural deprivation and a well-made point that IT offers the only means of maintaining the position of public libraries in a new age. Lastly, two people asked for the questionnaire to be on disk next time!

If the comments in this section of the survey tell us one thing it is that information technology features high on the agendas of the majority of public library services in the UK. Despite the apparent financial pressures that we all face, service managers are considering a wide range of developments. In fact more than ever before it is possible to see a sense of shared direction emerging across the country. The library management system is almost ubiquitous and once installed, libraries are continuing to enhance their systems by extending their scope or functionality – more libraries connected, automated acquisitions, etc. The Internet as a publicly accessible information resource may not have been widely accessible in June 1997, but if the intentions reported in this chapter are accurate, the level of penetration of the public Internet terminal must be increasing rapidly. Ditto for public access to CD-ROM, which is rightly becoming an essential tool in the resources of every public library. All of this lends support to the potential proposed for The People's Network and National Grid for Learning developments. By and large the public library service, despite resource difficulties, has recognized that future roles will depend on the effective use of information technology.

When you next look over the parapet at what IT developments are taking place within your local authority, reflect on the message of this chapter. Here we have an under resourced service which runs some of the most sophisticated realtime IT systems in local government; systems that are expected to run six, sometimes seven days a week and deal with levels of transactions matched more by supermarkets than by other local government systems. Many of these systems (library management, CD-ROM networks, Internet, Websites) are maintained in house and are now extending to become the engines for corporate information services. That is very different to the library service I entered a mere 30 years ago. Then the service may have been just as cherished by the users, but was almost always low down on the pecking order within the council. If your library remains in that position now it will soon be an exception.

We now have prime ministers and secretaries of state hailing our future role as agents for the information society. We must now all do that locally to get across the message that the public library is the engine of change for the masses. There is enough evidence contained within the comments analysed in this chapter to show the momentum that is building up, so let us all celebrate it as much as we can. Nobody would argue that it is always easy to make things work they way they should. A circulation system that crashes at the busiest time of the week is not likely to be popular, but if you can remember doing it, how popular were you when you dropped a whole tray of Browne issue?

REFERENCES

1 Gallimore, Alec, *Developing an IT strategy for your library*, London, Library Association Publishing, 1997.

6

Conclusions

What does it all mean? Five chapters of analysis, some parts perhaps more gripping than others, but like it or not a range of data reflecting the IT activities that were taking place in UK public libraries in the second half of 1997. It is tempting to try and draw general conclusions that paint a picture of the average library service, maybe even the average library. To the extent that the data allows us to do that thought experiment, the 'average library' might give some sort of datum to measure ourselves against. We must be cautious.

Averageness can be measured in a number of ways. If you have ten people five feet tall and ten seven feet tall, taking the mean average would suggest that most people were six feet tall. The maker of clothing for such as group, using the simple calculation of adding all the heights and dividing by the number of people would find few takers for the resulting clothes for six footers! A foolish analogy – who would do such a silly calculation? Who indeed? The problem we have, however, in trying to establish the IT usage of the average public library is that we cannot line them all up side by side to measure them, and even if we could it would be impossible to see the complexity of the total organization. We would have to make judgments about how one library service compared with another in terms of geography, staffing, policies and funding and so on. This is the sort of benchmarking dilemma constantly facing organizations such as the Audit Commission and CIPFA. How do you compare an apple with a pear?

Having said all of that, we can focus on averageness to the extent that we can take a shot at defining the applications likely to be found in most or some libraries: the applications you stand a good chance of seeing when you walk into your local library. That would help to give some sense of what is being done and what priorities are being set. We must remember that there is no national plan at present for the development of public library services, and therefore no nationally coordinated direction for the exploration and implementation of IT systems. If there is convergence of approach it is almost universally the result of an organic process of trial and error, initiative, sharing good ideas (and hopefully bad ones) and awareness of trends within the information and communication technologies sector. Things are set to change and it may be helpful to summarize at the beginning of this chapter just what the point of departure for the National Grid/People's Network will be.

Let me start to amplify the idea of the 'launch pad position' by reminding you about the take up of the systems described between Chapters 1 and 3. Those chapters covered the library management system, the use of electronic information services including the Internet and the role of the public library as an agent for open learning in it widest sense (more on that later in this chapter). I have extracted the most significant findings of those chapters and they are presented as a simple summary in Table 6.1.

Table 6.1 *Takeup of applications*

Application	Percentage takeup
Automated circulation (LMS)	95%
Automated circulation in all libraries	38%
OPAC	75%
Service points with OPAC	48%
Automated acquisitions	76%
CD-ROM (staff or public)	96%
CD-ROM (public use)	85%
Service points with public CD-ROM access	26%
Authorities with Internet access	74%
Service points with Internet access	9%
Service point with public Internet access	5%
Automated community information	77%
Public access micros	73%
Service points with public access micros	6%
Service points with open learning PCs	9%

Some trends stand out very clearly. While touched on individually in previous chapters, it will be helpful to use this summary table as a means of re-enforcing the patterns which the data highlight.

Starting at the top of the table and working down, the library management system is now a standard piece of the public library landscape in the same way that Browne issue once was in the past. All but a tiny minority of UK library services have automated circulation systems operating somewhere within their empires and, if the future plans section of Chapter 5 is to be believed, with serious commitment to extend access to as many libraries as possible. Thirty-eight percent of public libraries have already done just that and connected all their service points to a real time network for circulation. Do not go assuming that the 38% is evenly spread. The greatest chance of finding a service point connected to a library management system for circulation is in London, where the average is more than twice that elsewhere. Next come the English metropolitans. The obvious inference must be that automated circulation is most cost effective in the urban setting where distances are short and the level of use in the majority of service points is high enough to justify the installation of an automated system everywhere – it is not worth leaving the quieter libraries out of the system. Given the widely distributed communities of many rural areas and the small size of the population, it is not in any way surprising that networking the library management system has not spread as comprehensively as in urban situations.

It is likely that the same is true for the OPAC. The OPAC is now a popular means of delivering catalogue information: three-quarters of library authorities have one, while almost half of the service points in the UK have OPAC terminals. If there was ever a commitment shown by librarians to information technology it is manifest in the implementation of the OPAC. Having an OPAC is not like making the decision to provide access to CD-ROMs. The latter merely requires some money and some technical skills; building an OPAC from scratch is no mean task. The conversion process may only be done once, but it remains a mammoth task. And maintaining OPACs, while the need for cataloguers inhouse has diminished significantly as bibliographic records in electronic form become readily available to import from external sources, still calls for great care and attention to detail if the result is going to be useful to the ordinary customer.

I will not go step by step through the rest of the numbers in Table 6.1. The main trend which is apparent in the rest of the figures is the contrast between the high numbers of authorities providing public access to IT resources and the low number of service points at which those applications are provided. Seventy-four percent of library authorities may have Internet, but only 5% of service points in the UK offer public access. Ditto for public access micros and open learning. This represents quite slow diffusion of the technologies so far as public access is concerned. I do not find any of that very surprising. There is a very great difference between having an account with an internet service provider that costs just a few pounds each month and allows the odd librarian to surf, and the high-bandwidth connections that will be needed to connect libraries (and other public service points) across whole authorities to a range of resources, including the Internet. Both strategies are visible in public libraries across the UK and while *New library: the people's network*[1] paints a picture of high bandwidth networks connecting all public libraries together, today's reality is that such connectivity is very uncommon.

So, to return to my original question – whether or not some sort of 'average' public library can be sighted out there somewhere. There are several. The average central/district/town library will have access to a library management system, will provide OPAC terminals, may well have public access CD-ROM and possibly public access micros, which might just let customers access the Internet. An average medium sized urban library will have a library management system, an OPAC and maybe CD-ROM; the average rural library will have hardly any of that. At best there will be online access to the circulation system and an OPAC, but more likely nothing. A few will have public access CD-ROM, standalone rather than networked. Of course, there are exceptions, such as counties serving rural communities where all the service points are connected by high bandwidth networking, but they are unusual.

The landscape we have explored has been evolving and growing for more than 25 years. It has been an organic process which has allowed marginal changes to produce what is now a completely new picture seen from our vantage point. I have commented on a number of occasions in the past that for all of that development the customer going into any library for the first time in 20 years will not feel very lost or alienated. Things will be much as they were. Computers, maybe, but the main feature will be books and people. The books will be checked out supermarket style and the catalogue could be digital, but the feel of the place will be much as it was on the last visit 20 years ago. There are exceptions. Huyton Library close to Liverpool has on its top deck a large telecentre with over 30 PCs available for public use. The telecentre forms half of the reference service – the other half which is adjacent is books. When I visited, all of the terminals were in use and nobody was using the reference books. Downstairs people were happily borrowing books and I am sure there are times when the reference resources are alive with avid readers. There is in this an important point which we must not miss.

We are confronted by choices which are sometimes difficult to make. The evidence I see suggests that as a community resource the public library service is about to face some of the most dramatic changes of its long and honourable existence. The choices which will emerge are not about information technology OR books; not about community recycling (we call it lending) OR giving away information in digital packets; not about throwing away the stability and continuity that public libraries offer to their communities. The choices are about responding to the changing needs and opportunities and most significant of all signing up to a new style of service development. We have been able to respond to changing need before, indeed we do it all the time as we adjust our services to meet the needs of our communities. What we have never really done is sign up to true coordination of development and that is something which is both implicit and explicit in The People's Network and the National Grid for Learning. That is a new challenge.

We will be expected to adjust our service priorities to align with these networks and probably adjust our spending priorities to ensure that the hardware needed to deliver wide public access is in place. (I cannot believe that funding will come centrally for everything.) There is a longer term challenge in that we will not be the free agents we are now. As a professional group we pride ourselves on our cooperativeness. We lend our books to one other, we try to buy books cooperatively, and in some places there appears to be a genuine commitment to the principle that we can do better together what we do normally on our own. Information North, the cooperative of library authorities in the North East seems to be an example of this. However, I would argue that much of this has been at the margins of service management and has all been done on the basis of identifying tasks which have been attractive for all within the cooperative to share. If you look hard at some of the schemes of cooperative stock purchase you tend to find that while some library services follow their purchasing responsibilities to the letter, others either for lack of funds or lack of motivation do not. That is the weakness of the cooperative. There is usually no effective sanction on the minority by the majority. The current sovereignty of each local government unit guarantees it.

There is a paradox here which we must see clearly. We have developed and managed some of the most technically advanced public services in the country. Used by more people, available more than other services and probably with the most reliable systems (OK, on average!). We work together on projects such as EARL and through regional systems to create more for less. We are a profession with a lot of enthusiasm to develop further – you only need read thc comments in the appendices of Chapter 5 to see that there are plenty of ideas and seemingly the energy to get them moving. Agreed? But look at it another way, after 25 years of IT development in public libraries, how many shared library management systems are there? How many authorities have decided to club together to run a system together? The answer is very, very few. Indeed, where the new unitaries have appeared from previously-unified counties there are some hints that while sharing the existing library management system is unavoidable during the changeover period some of those new authorities are looking to 'go independent' at the earliest opportunity. There is the notable exception of the unitaries that have been created as a result of the break up of the county of Avon; CUBANs seems to be their nickname: Counties that Used to Be AvoN! These authorities continue to work with Somerset to select and implement a unified library management system that they will all share.

I come right back down now to the challenge I mentioned earlier. It is the need to face the future in a new way. We may not have the money but we have the technological skills to make the systems work. We even have some ideas about using them to the best advantage of our customers. What we must do is re-engineer our attitude to how we work together. We must never forget that all the lovely hardware is only of relevance to provide access to services, to information. It is as essential as shelving is to books, essential but invisible. Seeing hardware as digital shelving might help us to focus on the content. And this is the nub of the challenge. We cannot pick and choose about how we cooperate about the content that is available from our digital shelving. At present we can all scoot around the Internet for the price of a currant bun but in the future things will be different. Network access may be cheap, but the resources that are there to be harvested will be treated as commodities in the same way that we buy books today. We will need to be as one for several reasons.

First of all, the economies of scale to be gained from negotiating together are already demonstrable. The academic network JANET has an agency mandated to negotiate bulk discounts from Internet-based hosts. This means that any user who is authorized obtains access at a knock-down rate, certainly less than you or I would currently pay for access to the same information. The second reason reflects one of the most significant changes that our world will face. Until now we have not been large-scale creators of information ourselves. Community information has been our main territory and we have provided a unique service. The primary function of networking is to collect things together without actually moving them around or creating copies of those things, if you see what I mean. If the public library is to play a central role within the emerging information society it will be as much about creating information and mentoring users as about the shape of the technological systems that make those activities possible.

EARL (Electronic Access to Resources in Libraries) demonstrates the transition of the public library from simple storehouse of other people's information into mediator of access and coordinator of resources. EARL, which is a cooperative of almost 150 UK public library authorities presents an important exemplar of the public library as proactive agent for change. EARL is about building content in forms that are relevant to the users of public library services. That means how people in libraries go about tracing resources across networks as well as people remote from libraries accessing the resources of public libraries in their quest for knowledge. Content will be everything. If the new networks do not meet real need, do not make the lives of people better and more fulfilled, then the projected benefits of the information society will not arise. That implies understanding what content is important and how it should be packaged. IT also means the public library must be closely involved in the act of creation. I do not suggest that we should produce everything, rather that we have knowledge of the needs of our communities which must influence the nature and range of the content.

The final reason for a closer collaboration is the most telling. We are at a point of change, when the tradition of voluntary, sometimes arbitrary, cooperation will have to be swept aside as government policy lays down much more closely how our services should develop in the information age. There will be a quid pro quo that central funding will require our commitment to common objectives and practices. A national network will demand standard systems and resources and we should welcome that. Like many other professional groups, particularly those within the public sector, being part of the information society movement means learning a new language of behaviour. The results of the 1997 survey show quite clearly that we are not generally afraid of the technology: we are prepared to use IT when appropriate and when the money is there. However, the next step, for us and the other adventurers around us, is a big one. Giving up some of the independence we have had in our feudal states where we have been able to decide the direction and priorities of service will be hard for some people. Similarly recognizing that the work that EARL has started is but the first hint of what the future landscape will be like will mean some radical rethinking of our resource deployment.

I have argued in more places than I care to remember that public libraries have a chance to place themselves centre stage within the information society; the 'heart and the brain of the information society' was the expression I used. It was not idle rhetoric. We already have a strong position within our communities; we have adapted better than most other services to the needs and opportunities offered by IT and there is much enthusiasm. We are not so experienced at the creation of content or the ways in which networks will open up new vistas for our customers. Coming back to the point just made above, we have never really had strong direction nationally. Those are our challenges.

Let me close this chapter with two practical examples of how the public library, coordinated nationally and exploiting the benefits of networking could add significant value to some of the things we already do. Start with community information. We saw in Chapter 2 that libraries across the country are carving a variety of routes into the future. Each building a database, managing it and using a variety of technologies to disseminate the information. It is a unique service which few are likely to want to emulate. It costs a lot to do and the economic value of each individual piece of information is small. Few would pay a significant amount of money to find out about a particular club or group; yet the community benefit of having such systems it high. Community information is therefore an expensive product which will never produce a return worth commercial investment. The other obvious point to make is that community information is local. We do not frequently share our databases regionally, let alone nationally. That has always seemed rather strange to me. The fact that local information exists is of value to anyone interested in that community. So, if you are travelling to Edinburgh you may well benefit from searching the community information database from Los Angeles, Thornton Heath, wherever.

Many public libraries have now switched their community information to the Web so that it is available to anyone, anywhere. At the moment that drift is patchy and there is no coordination between different places. Just suppose we could cooperate enough to create one database nationally, with standard formats and Web-based. There could still be local management of data, but now anyone could search and find, say, archery clubs across South London, or indeed, find all the clubs nationally. This could be a very powerful resource for tourism, both allowing interaction between neighbouring library services and the promotion of local resources nationally. The key factor of course is that we all have to accept one national standard – like a national curriculum for community information. What could be wrong with that? To my mind nothing, but it comes back to learning the language of the future.

Another brief example comes to mind from the domain of lifelong learning, which I touched on in Chapter 3. I referred in that chapter to the need for educationalists (and for us) to recognize that lifelong learning is not simply about getting everyone into Open University type activity – gaining qualifications and reskilling. They are vital to a developing workforce, and the University for Industry, for example, could find as other institutions have done in the past, that the public library is a key outlet for those and other traditional learning experiences. The university is dead, long live the public library! Yet we will never be in a position to replace the skills of the educationalist. We can offer a new home, but we will have to learn ourselves to cooperate not just with our peers but with other professionals: the public library as the workplace of many different skills – advisers, teachers, interpreters of information and librarians.

Lifelong learning is more than that. Restructuring the phrase as ‘learning for life’ suggests a rather different slant, as I stated in Chapter 3. This is an area where we can be bullish. We have a great deal of knowledge about people who are in need of small pieces of information to make their lives better, who have needs which no educationalist would ever describe as a learning deficit: the plant to be identified, the phone number, the book which recaptures a long forgotten memory. We need to shout very loud about this during the coming years lest our chance to shine in these trivial yet important things is drowned by the din being made by those people who see the national network as solely an engine for promoting a new model for education.

When I started to work on this chapter, I intended that it should present something of a comparative study. Anything which has a European or global dimension is bound to attract a few more sales. Somehow the organic style of writing which had led us to this point seems to have avoided the topic of other countries. I can say for sure that overall we are not the technically most advanced public libraries in the world. Go to Denmark and you will see greater investment in the technical development of public libraries. It is an impressive sight to visit a Danish public library and see almost 70 public access Internet terminals – all free of charge. Many other parts of Scandinavia have developed highly advanced IT systems within their libraries. In Finland there is a move to provide all citizens with an e-mail address for life and to use the public library as the agent for provision of the addresses. The recent study by McClure, et al.[1] reports that in 1997, 60% of US public libraries surveyed provided public access in one or more service points. We are not then ahead of the game.

True, but I feel we have a great chance to leap ahead if the People's Network/National Grid for Learning become reality and if we as agents for change can think clearly and altruistically enough to change not just the things around us, but change ourselves. It is not over dramatic to suggest that there is a revolution coming which will require us to alter many of our traditional values. We must be prepared to respond. On occasions I use the analogy of progress as moving through a landscape which may be fully visible close at hand and behind, but ahead is frequently blurred. We hack a path along routes we think will be of benefit and sometimes cross the paths of others. Just occasionally we get a glimpse of the scenery further ahead. Now is such a time. We must clear the paths together and work towards that new landscape to ensure it is a good place for everyone to be. In the words of one revolutionary – 'May a thousand flowers bloom.'

REFERENCE

1 *New library: the people's network*, Library and Information Commission, 1997.

2 McClure, C. R., Berdot, J. C., and Fletcher, P. D., *1997 national survey of US public libraries and the Internet*, American Library Association Office for Technology Policy.

Contacts

ABERDEEN
W Thomson
Central Library
Rosemount Viaduct
ABERDEEN
AB25 1GW
Tel. 01224-652518
Fax 01224-641985

ABERDEENSHIRE
Ian Strachan
Lib and Info Service
Meldrum Meg Way
OLD MELDRUM
AB51 0 GN
Tel. 01651-872107
Tel. 01651-872142

ANGLESEY
Mr Sion Caffell
Llangefni Library
Lon-y-felin
LLANGEFNI
LL77 7RT
Tel. 01248-752028
Fax 01248-750365
Sion@llyfrlib.demon.co.uk

ANGUS
G N Drummond
County buildings
Market Street
FORFAR
DD8 3WF
Tel. 01307-473-256
Fax 01307-462-590

ARGYLL AND BUTE
A I Ewan
Library HQ
Highland Avenue
DUNOON
PA23 8PB
Tel. 01369-703214
Fax 01369-703214

BARKING AND DAGENHAM
Alan Hill
Central Library
BARKING
IG11 7NB
Tel. 0181-517 8666
Fax 0181-594 1156
fm019@viscount.org.uk

BARNET
Richard Nurse
Educational Services
Friern Barnet Lane
LONDON
N11 3DL
Tel. 0181-359 2297
Fax 0181-359 2788
fb16@dial.pipex.com

BARNSLEY
S Bashforth
Central Library
Shambles Street
BARNSLEY
S70 2JF
Tel. 01226-773927
Fax 01226-773955
Librarian@Barnsley.ac.uk

BATH & N.E. SOMERSET
Richard Ashby
Northgate House
Upper Borough Walls
BATH
BA1 1RG
Tel. 01225-396404
Fax 01225-396461
Richard-Ashby@Bathnes.gov.uk

BEDFORDSHIRE

Andy Baker
Leisure Services
County Hall
BEDFORD
MK42 9AP
Tel. 01234-228301
Fax 01234-228921
bedlibres@cix.compulink.co.uk

BERKSHIRE

Wilma Grant
Shire Hall
Shinfield Park
READING
RG2 9XD
Tel. 0118-923 3237

BEXLEY

Pam Horton
Library Service
Hill View Drive
WELLING
DA16 3RY
Tel. 01322-553 665
Fax 01322-553 665

BIRMINGHAM

Brian Gambles
Baskerville House
Broad Street
BIRMINGHAM
B1 2NE
Tel. 0121-235 3372
Fax 0121-233 9702
brian.gambles@dial.pipex.com

BLAENAU GWENT

Steve Hardman
Festival House
Victoria Business Park
EBBW VALE
NP3 6EX
Tel. 01495-355318
Fax 01495-355468
steve.bg.libs@dial.pipex.com

BOLTON

Marguerite Gracey
Central Library
Le Mans Crescent
BOLTON
BL1 1SE
Tel. 01204-522311 x2167
Fax 01204-363224

BOURNEMOUTH

Malcolm Wood
Town Hall
BOURNEMOUTH
BH2 6DY
Tel. 01202-454618
Fax 01202-454620

BRADFORD

Michael Walmsley
Central Library
Prince's Way
BRADFORD
BD1 1NN
Tel. 01274-753544
Fax 01274-395108
michael.walmsley@
bradford.gov.uk

BRENT

Lorna Brown
Chesterfield house
9, Park Lane
WEMBLEY
HA9 7RW
Tel. 0181-937 3149
Fax 0181-937 3023
lorna.brown@brent.gov.uk

BRIDGEND

Kath Ewins
Library HQ
Coed Parc
BRIDGEND
CF31 4BA
Tel. 01656-767451
Fax 01656-645719
blis@bridgendlib.gov.uk

BRIGHTON AND HOVE

Sally McMahon
Central Library
Church Street
BRIGHTON
BN1 1UE
Tel. 01273-296963
Fax 01273-296965
SMcMahon@dial.pipex.com

BRISTOL

Robert Harrison
Central Library
College Green
BRISTOL
BS1 5TL
Tel. 0117-927 6121 x231
Fax 0117-922 6775

BROMLEY

Gerry Traynor
Central Library
High Street
BROMLEY
BR1 1EX
Tel. 0181-460 9955
Fax 0181-313 0475
bromley-cenlib@cityscape.co.uk

BUCKINGHAMSHIRE

Brenda Ponton
County Library
Walton Street
AYLESBURY
HP20 1UU
Tel. 01296-383109
Fax 01296-382259
bponton@buckscc.gov.uk

BURY

Peter J Morgan
Leisure Services Department,
Textile Hall
Manchester Road
BURY
BL9 0DR
Tel. 0161-253 5877
Fax 0161-253 5857

CAERPHILLY
Mary Palmer
County Library HQ
County Hall
CWMBRAN
NP44 2XL
Tel. 01443-864963
Fax 01443-864941

CALDERDALE
Malcolm Corbett
Central Library
Northgate
HALIFAX
HX1 1UN
Tel. 01422-392628
Fax 01422-392615
calderdale@geo2.poptel.org.uk

CAMBRIDGESHIRE
Mike Hoskings
Babbage House
Shire Hall
CAMBRIDGE
CB3 0AP
Tel. 01223-717063
Fax 01223-717079
mike.hosking@libraries.
camcnty.gov.uk

CAMDEN
Lawrence Morgan
The Crowndale Centre
218 Eversholt Street
LONDON
NW1 1BD
Tel. 0171-911 1613
Fax 0171-911 1543

CARDIFF
Central Library
Frederick Street
CARDIFF
CF1 4DT
Tel. 01222-382116
Fax 01222-238642

CARMARTHENSHIRE
David F Griffiths
County Library
Furnace House
CARMARTHEN
SA31 1LN
Tel. 01267-238584

CEREDIGION
William H Howells
Public Library
Corporation Street
ABERYSTWYTH
SY23 2BU
Tel. 01970-617464
Fax 01970-625059

CHESHIRE
Ray Benton
Goldsmith House
Hamilton Place
CHESTER
CH1 1SE
Tel. 01244-606024
Fax 01244-602805
bentonr@cheshire.gov.uk

CITY OF LONDON
Cathy Pringle
Guildhall Library
Aldermanbury
LONDON
EC2P 2EJ
Tel. 0171-333 1879
Fax 0171-600 3384
cathy.pringle@ms.
corpotlondon.gov.uk

CLACKMANNANSHIRE
Alloa Library
26 Drysdale Street
ALLOA
FK10 JL
Tel. 01259-722262

CONWY
Conwy County Borough Council
Bodlondeb
CONWY
LL30 2RP
Tel. 01492-576140
Fax 01492-592114
raldrich.library@llanduduo.co.uk

CORNWALL
Marilyn Gay
County Hall
TRURO
TR1 3AY
Tel. 01872-271352
Fax 01872-223772

COVENTRY
Bob Sidney
Spire House
New Union Street
COVENTRY
CV1 2PS
Tel. 01203-832317
Fax 01203-833163
covinfo@discover.co.uk

CROYDON
Chris Batt
Croydon Clocktower
Katharine Street
CROYDON
CR9 1ET
Tel. 0181-253 1000
Fax 0181-253 1004
lbcbatt@croydon.gov.uk

CUMBRIA
Alan Welton
County Library, Arroyo Block
The Castle
CARLISLE
CA3 8XF
Tel. 01228-607307
Fax 01228-607299

DARLINGTON
L Litchfield
Central Library
Crown Street
DARLINGTON
DL1 1ND
Tel. 01325-461320

DENBIGHSHIRE
R Arwyn Jones
County Hall
MOLD
CH7 6GR
Tel. 01824-706767
Fax 01824-706775
ou83@dial.pipex.com

DERBY
Ulla Panes
Central Library
Wardwick
DERBY
DE1 1HF
Tel. 01332-716609
Fax 01332-715549

DERBYSHIRE
David Swarbrick
County Hall
MATLOCK
DE4 3AG
Tel. 01629-580000 x6584
Fax 01629-585363
derbys_libraries@globalnet.co.uk

DEVON
Roy Eden
Barley House
Isleworth Road
EXETER
EX4 1RQ
Tel. 01392-384328
Fax 01392-384316
reden@mf.devon_cc.gov.uk

DONCASTER
John Mellor
PO Box 270
College Road
DONCASTER
DN1 3JE
Tel. 01302-722327
Fax 01302-727293

DORSET
Norman Shirley
County Library HQ
Colliton Park
DORCHESTER
DT1 1XJ
Tel. 01305-224458
Fax 01305-224344

DUDLEY
Chris Wrigley
Dudley Library
St James's Road
DUDLEY
DY1 1HR
Tel. 01384-815552
Fax 01384-815543

DUMFRIES AND GALLOWAY
H McArthur
Central Support Unit
Catherine Street
DUMFRIES
DG1 1JB
Tel. 01387-253820
Fax 01387-260294
libs&I@dumgal.gov.uk

DUNDEE
Pamela Tulloch
Tayside House
Critchton Street
DUNDEE
DD1 3RR
Tel. 01382-434336
Fax 01382-434642
ptulloch@tagnet.co.uk

DURHAM
Andy Raine
County Hall
DURHAM
DH1 5TY
Tel. 0191-383 3719
Fax 0191-384 1336
agraine@durham.gov.uk

EALING
Peter Hounsell
Library Admin
14 Uxbridge Road
LONDON
W5 2HL
Tel. 0181-810 7650
Fax 0181-810 7651

EAST AYRSHIRE
Mrs Elaine Gray
Dick Institute
14 Elmbank Avenue
KILMARNOCK
KA1 3BU
Tel. 01563-526401
Fax 01563-529661
dick_institute@compuserve.com

E. DUMBARTONSHIRE
Elaine Fulton
Central Library
2 West High St
KIRKINTILLOCH
G66 1AD
Tel. 0141-776 5666
Fax 0141-776 0408

EAST LOTHIAN
David Moody
Library and Museum HQ
Dunbar Road
HADDINGTON
EH41 3PJ
Tel. 01620-828202
Fax 01620-828201
HQ@clothlib.

EAST RENFREW
Mr J Hutcheon
Cultural Services
Glen Street
BARRHEAD
G78 1QA
Tel. 0141-577 3511
Fax 0141-577 3501

EAST RIDING
Alan Moir
Council Office
BEVERLEY
HU17 9BA
Tel. 01482-884984
amoir@erlis.karoo.co.uk

EAST SUSSEX

Gavin Wright
County Library HQ
Southdown House
LEWES
BN7 ISQ
Tel. 01273-481874
Fax 01273-480092

EDINBURGH

Maggie Corr
Central Library
George IV Bridge
EDINBURGH
EH1 1EG
Tel. 0131-225 5584 x227
Fax 0131-225 8783

ENFIELD

Andy Castro
Civic Centre
Silver Street
ENFIELD
EN1 3XA
Tel. 0181-967 9375
Fax 0181-982 7378
andy.castro@dial.pipex.com

ESSEX

Martin Hole
County Library HQ
Golday Gardens
CHELMSFORD
CM2 0EW
Tel. 01245-284981
Fax 01245-490199
libmsu@essexcc.gov.uk

FALKIRK

S Allison
Victoria Buildings
Queen Street
FALKIRK
FK2 7AF
Tel. 01324 506802
Fax 01324 506801

FIFE

Dorothy Miller
Arts, Libraries and Museums
Town House
KIRKCALDY
KY1 1XW
Tel. 01592-412940
Fax 01592-412941

FLINTSHIRE

L Rawsthorne
Library HQ
County Hall
MOLD
CH7 6NW
Tel. 01352-704400
Fax 01352-753662
flintslib@dial.pipex.com

GATESHEAD

Ian Hunter
Central Library
Prince Consort Road
GATESHEAD
NE8 4LN
Tel. 0191-477 3478
Fax 0191-477 7454
hunter@gateslib.demon.co.uk

GLASGOW

Andrew Miller
The Mitchell Library
North Street
GLASGOW
G3 7DN
Tel. 0141-287 2809

GLOUCESTERSHIRE

Liz Buckle
Quayside House
Shire Hall
GLOUCESTER
GL1 2HY
Tel. 01452-425373
Fax 01452-425042
clams@gloscc.gov.uk

GREENWICH

John Morgan
Leisure Services
147 Powis Street
LONDON
SE18 6JL
Tel. 0181-317 4466
Fax 0181-317 4868

GWYNEDD

Mr T Hywel James
Caernarfon Library
Pavilion Hill
CAERNARFON
LL55 1SH
Tel. 01286-679465
Fax 01286-671137

HACKNEY

Stephen Allberry
Shoreditch Town Hall
380 Old Street
LONDON
EC1V 9LT
Tel. 0181-442 5237
Fax 0181-525 2579
sallberry@hackney.gov.uk

HAMMERSMITH AND FULHAM

John Aquilina
Hammersmith Library
Shepherds Bush Road
LONDON
W6 7AT
Tel. 0181-576 5055
Fax 0181-576 5022
FLR@HAFLIBS.ORG.UK

HAMPSHIRE

John Haylock
County Library HQ
81 North Walls
WINCHESTER
SO23 8BY
Tel. 01962-846089
Fax 01962-856615
libsjh@hants.gov.uk

HARINGEY

Jean Earley
Central Library
High Road
LONDON
N22 6XD
Tel. 0181-888 1291
Fax 0181-889 0110

HARROW

Nikki Copleston
Civic Centre Library
Civic Centre
HARROW
HA1 2UU
Tel. 0181-424 1046
Fax 0181-424 1971
ncoplest.educatio@harrow.gov.uk

HARTLEPOOL

Central Library
124 York Road
HARTLEPOOL
TS26 9DE
Tel. 01429-272905
Fax 01429-275685
reflib@hartlepool.gov.uk

HAVERING

Mrs P Vickers
Central Library
St Edwards Way
ROMFORD
RM1 3AR
Tel. 01708-2386
Fax 01708-2391

HEREFORD AND WORCESTER

Brian Brumhead
County Hall
Spetchley Road
WORCESTER
WR5 2NP
Tel. 01905-766236

HERTFORDSHIRE

Andrew Cross
Libraries, Arts, Info
New Barnfield
HATFIELD
AL10 9XG
Tel. 01707-281542
Fax 01707-281548
andrew.cross@hertacc.gov.uk

HIGHLAND

Christopher Phillips
Library Support Unit
31a Harbour Street
INVERNESS
IV1 1UA
Tel. 01463-235713
Fax 01463-236986

HILLINGDON

Duncan Westlake
Libraries Service
Central Library
UXBRIDGE
UB8 1HD
Tel. 01895-250710
Fax 01895-811164
dwesltah@lbhill.gov.uk

HOUNSLOW

Geoffrey Allen
Civic Cenre
Lampton Road
HOUNSLOW
TW3 4DN
Tel. 0181-862 5797

INVERCLYDE

G McGilvray
Central Library
Clyde Square
GREENOCK
PA15 1NA
Tel. 01475-726211
Fax 01475-730185

ISLE OF WIGHT

Tim Blackmore
Culture and Leisure
The Guildhall
NEWPORT
PO30 1TY
Tel. 01983-823822
Fax 01983-823841
tim.blackmore@virgin.net

ISLINGTON

Val Dawson
Library Services
227/229 Essex Road
LONDON
N1 3PW
Tel. 0171-4773868
Fax 0171-4773873
valdawson@dial.pipex.com

KENSINGTON AND CHELSEA

Geoff Boulton
Central Library
Phillimore Walk
LONDON
W8 7RX
Tel. 0171-361 3060
Fax 0171-361 2976
libghb@rbkc.gov.uk

KENT

Patrick Browne
Library HQ
Springfield
MAIDSTONE
ME14 2LH
Tel. 01622-605200
Fax 01622-605292

KINGSTON UPON HULL

Miss J Shaw
Central Library
Albion Street
KINGSTON UPON HULL
HU1 3TF
Tel. 01482-883040
Fax 01482-883080

KINGSTON UPON THAMES

Simon Cooper
Kingston Library
Fairfield Road
KINGSTON
KT1 2PS
Tel. 0181-547 6420
Fax 0181-547 6411

KIRKLEES

Rob Liarburton
Cultural Services HQ
Red Doles Lane
HUDDERSFIELD
HD2 1YF
Tel. 01484-226340
Fax 01484-226342
Hq@geo2.poptel.org.uk

KNOWSLEY

Miss Vicky Feltham
PO Box 22
Archway Road
HUYTON
LN1 1YL
Tel. 0151-482 1307
Fax 0151-482 1304

LAMBETH

Carol Holmes
Courtenay House
9-15 New Park Road
LONDON
SW2 4DU
Tel. 0171-926 7198
Fax 0171-926 0161

LANCASHIRE

Mr Graham Dunbar
County Library
143 Corporation Street
PRESTON
PR1 2UQ
Tel. 01772-264024
Fax 01772-264880
lancs-co-lib-hq
@mcri.poptel.co.uk

LEEDS

Patricia Carroll
Leisure Services
The Headrow
LEEDS
LS1 3AD
Tel. 0113-214 3314
Fax 0113-214 3339
patricia.carroll@leeds.gov.uk

LEICESTER

Michael Clark
New Walk Centre
Welford Place
LEICESTER
LE1 6ZG
Tel. 0116-252 6762
Fax 0116-252 9257

LEICESTERSHIRE

P Love
County Hall
Glenfield
LEICESTER
LE3 8SS
Tel. 0116-265 7376
Fax 0116-265 7370
plove@leics.gov.uk

LEWISHAM

Vaughan Whibley
Education/Comm Serv
Laurence House
Catford
SE6 4RU
Tel. 0181-695 6000 x8002
Fax 0181-690 4387

LINCOLNSHIRE

Ms Lorraine Jubb
County Offices
Newland
LINCOLN
LN1 1YL
Tel. 01522-553207
Fax 01522-552811

LIVERPOOL

Alan Metcalf
Steers House
Canning Place
LIVERPOOL
L1 8HN
Tel. 0151-225 5403
Fax 0151-225 5401

LUTON

J George
Central Library
St George's Square
LUTON
LU1 2NG
Tel. 01582-730161
Fax 01582-724638

MANCHESTER

Andrew Jackson
Central Library
St Peter's Square
MANCHESTER
M2 5PD
Tel. 0161-234 1924
Fax 0161-234 1963
100440.3546@compuserve.com

MERTHYR TYDFIL

G James
Central Library
High Street
MERTHYR TYDFIL
CF47 8AF
Tel. 01685-723057
Fax 01685-370696

MERTON

Rosemary Doyle
Civic Centre
London Road
MORDEN
SM4 5DX
Tel. 0181-545 3772
Fax 0181-545 4037

MIDDLESBROUGH

Neil Bennett
Central Library
Victoria Square
MIDDLESBROUGH
TS1 2AYL
Tel. 01642-263350
Fax 01642-230690

MIDLOTHIAN

Annie Manager
Library HQ
2 Clerk Street
LOANHEAD
EH20 9DR
Tel. 0131-440 2210
Fax 0131-440 4635
mc-libhq-blossoming@
compuserve.com

MILTON KEYNES

W Pearson
Central Library
555 Silbury Boulevard
MILTON KEYNES
MK9 2HL
Tel. 01908-835010
Fax 01908-835085

MONMOUTHSHIRE

Peter Gaw
Floor 5
County Hall
CWMBRAN
NP44 2XB
Tel. 01633-644551
Fax 01633-644545
mlis@dial.pipex.com

MORAY

G A Campbell
Council Office
High Street
ELGIN
IV30 1BX
Tel. 01343-563398
Fax 01343-563410

N. IRELAND BELFAST

J N Montgomery
Central Library
Royal Avenue
BELFAST
BT1 1EA
Tel. 01232-243233
Fax 01232-332819

N. IRELAND NORTH EASTERN

Brian Cooper
Area Library HQ
Demesne Avenue
BALLYMENA
BT43 7BG
Tel. 01266-664102
Fax 01266-632038
BrianCooper@POBOXES.com

N. IRELAND SOUTH EASTERN

Noel Sloan
Library HQ
Windmill Hill
BALLYNAHINCH
BT24 8DH
Tel. 01238-566421
Fax 01238-565072

N. IRELAND SOUTHERN

Richard Burns
Library HQ
1 Markethill Road
ARMAGH
BT60 1NR
Tel. 01861-525353
Fax 01861-526879

N. IRELAND WESTERN

Rosemary Adams
Library HQ
1 Spillars Place
OMAGH
BT78 1HL
Tel. 01662-244821
Fax 01662-246716
librarian@omalib.demon.co.uk

NEATH AND PORT TALBOT

Lloyd Ellis
Reginald Street
Velindre
PORT TALBOT
SA13 1YY
Tel. 01639-899829
Fax 01639-899152
lloyd@nptlib.clara.net

NEWCASTLE UPON TYNE

Barbara Moorhead
Central Library
Princess Square
NEWCASTLE UPON TYNE
NE99 1DX
Tel. 0191-261 0691 ext241
Fax 0191-232 4904
moorhead@dial.pipex.com

NEWHAM

George Bye
East Ham Library
High Street South
LONDON
E8 4EL
Tel. 0181-472 1430 x21732
Fax 0181-557 8845
george.bye@newham.gov.uk

NEWPORT

Melanie Sheridan
Central Library
John Frost Square
NEWPORT
NP9 1PA
Tel. 01633-265539
Fax 01633-222615

NORFOLK

Miriam Robbins
County Hall
Martineau Lane
NORWICH
NR1 2DH
Tel. 01603-222395
Fax 01603-222422
miriam.robbins.lib@norfolk.
gov.uk

NORTH AYRSHIRE

A P Macnaughton
Library
39 Princes Street
ARDROSSAN
KA22 8BT
Tel. 01294-469137
Fax 01294-604236

N.E. LINCOLNSHIRE

John English
Central Library
Town Hall Square
GRIMSBY
DN31 1HG
Tel. 01472-323611
Fax 01472-323618

NORTH LANARKSHIRE

Buchanan Tower
Cumbernauld Road
STEPPS
G33 6HR
Tel. 01698-251311

NORTH LINCOLNSHIRE

Margaret Carr
PO Box 35
Station Road
BRIGG
DN20 8XJ
Tel. 01724-297253
Fax 01724-297258
jlc-lib@rmplc.co.uk

NORTH SOMERSET

Andy Brisley
PO Box 146
Town Hall
WESTON-S-MARE
BS23 1AE
Tel. 01275-873498
Fax 01275-343630

NORTH TYNESIDE

Fred Miller
Central Library
Northumberland Sq
NORTH SHIELDS
NE30 1QU
Tel. 0191-2005424
Fax 0191-2006118
FredM@ntlib.demon.co.uk

NORTH YORKSHIRE

Mr Chris Riley
County Library
Grammar School Lane
NORTHALLERTON
DL6 1DF
Tel. 01609-776271
Fax 01609-780793

NORTHAMPTONSHIRE

Eric Wright
PO Box 259
27 Guildhall Road
NORTHAMPTON
NN1 1BA
Tel. 01604-20262
Fax 01604-26789

NORTHUMBERLAND

Mike Dimelow
County Central Library
The Willows
MORPETH
NE6 1TA
Tel. 01670-511156
Fax 01670-518012
norcolib.demon.co.uk

NOTTINGHAMSHIRE

Nick London
Trent Bridge House
Fox Road
WEST BRIDGFORD
NG2 6BJ
Tel. 0115-985 4205
Fax 0115-928 6400
london_n@ls.nottscc.gov.uk

OLDHAM

Richard Lambert
Oldham Library
Union Street
OLDHAM
OL1 1DN
Tel. 0161-911 4632
Fax 0161-911 4630
richard.lib@oldham.gov.uk

ORKNEY

Karen Walker
Council Offices
School Place
KIRKWALL
KW15 1NW
Tel. 01856-873166
Fax 01856-815260

OXFORDSHIRE

Mike King
Central Library
Westgate
OXFORD
OX1 1DJ
Tel. 01865-810299
it.occdla@dial_pipex.com

PEMBROKESHIRE

Clive Richards
County Library
Dew Street
HAVERFORDWEST
SA61 1SU
Tel. 01437-775243
Fax 01437-769218

PERTH AND KINROSS

Mr M Moir
A K Bell Library
York Place
PERTH
PA2 8EP
Tel. 01738-444949
Fax 01738-477010

POOLE

Lyn Pullen
Central Library
Dolphin Centre
POOLE
BH15 1QE
Tel. 01202-673910
Fax 01202-670253

PORTSMOUTH

Colin Brown
Central Library
Guildhall Square
PORTSMOUTH
PO1 2DX
Tel. 01705-819311
Fax 01705-839855
clpmcb@hantsnet.hants.gov.uk

POWYS

Tudfil Adams
Powys Library HQ
Cefnllys Road
LLANDRINDOD W
LD1 5LD
Tel. 01597-826155

REDBRIDGE

Sarah Mears
Central Library
Clements Road
ILFORD
IG1 1EA
Tel. 0181-478 7145
Fax 0181-553 3299

REDCAR AND CLEVELAND

Carol Barnes
Cargo Fleet Offices
Middlesbrough Road
REDCAR
TS10 1XX
Tel. 01642-444357
Fax 01642-444341

RENFREWSHIRE

Jill Mckee
Library
Marchfield Avenue
PAISLEY
G78 1JB
Tel. 0141-887 2468
Fax 0141-848 0583

RHONDDA

Kathleen Langley
Education Centre
Grawen Street
PORTH
CF39 0JB
Tel. 01443-7773592
Fax 01443-777047

RICHMOND

Derrick Fernandes
Langholm Lodge
Petersham Road
RICHMOND
TW10 6UX
Tel. 0181-940 3691
Fax 0181-940 7516

ROCHDALE

Steven Hood
Wheatsheaf Library
Baillie Street
ROCHDALE
OL16 1JZ
Tel. 01706-864967
Fax 01706-864992

ROTHERHAM

Elenore Fisher
Library & Arts Centre
Walker Place
ROTHERHAM
S65 1JH
Tel. 01709-823614
Fax 01709-823650
elenore.fisher@rotherham.gov.uk

RUTLAND

Roy Knight
Libraries & Museums
Catmose Street
OAKHAM
LE15 6HW
Tel. 01572-723654
Fax 01572-757576

SALFORD

Robin Culpin
Vulcan House
Albion Place Crescent
SALFORD
M5 4NL
Tel. 0161-736 9448
Fax 0161-736 0429

SANDWELL

Barry Clark
Shaftsbury House
402 Highstreet
SANDWELL
B70 9LT
Tel. 0121-569 4908
Fax 0121-569 4907
dn025@viscount.org.uk

SCOTTISH BORDERS

John Beedle
Library HQ
St Mary's Mill
SELKIRK
TD7 5EW
Tel. 01750-20842
Fax 01750-22875
library1@netcomuk.co.uk

SEFTON

Roger Wall
Pavilion Buildings
99-105 Lord Street
SEFTON
PR8 1RJ
Tel. 0151-934 2372
Fax 0151-934 2370

SHEFFIELD

Dave Spencer
Central Library
Surrey Street
SHEFFIELD
S1 1XZ
Tel. 0114-273 4751
Fax 0114-273 5009
d.spencer@dial.pipex.com

SHETLAND ISLANDS

John G Hunter
Shetland Library
Lower Hillhead
LERWICK
ZE1 0EL
Tel. 01595-693868

SHROPSHIRE
Tim Williams
Column House
7 London Road
SHREWSBURY
SY2 6NW
Tel. 01743-255000

SOLIHULL
Hillary Halliday
Central Library
Homer Road
SOLIHULL
B91 3RG
Tel. 0121-704 8227
Fax 0121-704 6991

SOMERSET
John Powell
Library Administration
Mount Street
BRIDGWATER
TA6 3ES
Tel. 01278-451201
Fax 01278-425787
JRPowell@compuserve.com

SOUTH AYRSHIRE
Charles Deas
Library HQ
26 Green Street
AYR
KA8 8AD
Tel. 01292-288820
Fax 01292-619619

S. GLOUCESTERSHIRE
Linda Horne
Broad Lane Offices
Engine Common
YATE
BS17 5PN
Tel. 01454-865782
Fax 01454-281662

SOUTH LANARKSHIRE
Jean Keay
Central Library
The Olympia Centre
EAST KILBRIDE
G74 1PG
Tel. 01698-452598
Fax 01698-286334

SOUTH TYNESIDE
David Abbott
Central Library
Prince George Square
SOUTH SHIELDS
NE33 2PE
Tel. 0191-427 1717 x2100
Fax 0191-455 8085

SOUTHAMPTON
Liz Kotlarz
Central Library
Civic Centre
SOUTHAMPTON
SO14 7LW
Tel. 01703-833412
Fax 01703-336305
clsnek@hants.gov.uk

SOUTHWARK
Gill Butler
Education and Leisure
15 Spa Road
LONDON
SE16 3QW
Tel. 0171-525 1579
Fax 0171-525 1568

ST HELENS
Robin W Turvey
Town Hall
Corporation Street
ST HELENS
WA10 1DY
Tel. 01744-455409
Fax 01744-20836

STAFFORDSHIRE
Christine Langton
Library HA
Shire Hall
STAFFORD
ST17 4AY
Tel. 01785-278326
Fax 01785-278309
christine.langton@staffordshire.
gov.uk

STIRLING
A Muirhead
Library HQ
Borrowmeadow Road
STIRLING
FK7 7TN
Tel. 01786-432388
Fax 01786-432395

STOCKPORT
Richard Ayres
Stopford House
Piccadilly
STOCKPORT
SK1 3XE
Tel. 0161-474 4531

STOCKTON
Helen Dean
Central Library
Church Road
STOCKTON
TS18 1TU
Tel. 01642-393918
Fax 01642-393924
helen.dean@sbcssz.
stockton-bc.gov.uk

STOKE ON TRENT
Jo Toy
Hanley Library
Bethesda Street
STOKE ON TRENT
ST1 3RS
Tel. 01782-238406
Fax 01782-238499
jo.toy@stoke01.stoke-cc.gov.uk

SUFFOLK
M Johnson
St Andrew House
County Hall
IPSWICH
IP4 2JS
Tel. 01473-584577
Fax 01473-584549

SUNDERLAND

Ian Bower
Library & Arts Centre
Fawcett Street
SUNDERLAND
SR1 1RE
Tel. 0191-514 8441
Fax 0191-514 8444
ian@sund2.unity.libms.co.uk

SURREY

Susan Chamberlain
Surrey County Council
County Hall
COBHAM
KT1 2DN
Tel. 01932-860650
Fax 01932-862737
libclient@dial.pipex.com

SUTTON

Graham Dash
Central Library
St Nicholas Way
SUTTON
SM1 1EQ
Tel. 0181-770 4763
Fax 0181-770 4777
sutton.lib@dial.pipex.com

SWANSEA

Pauline Morris
County Library HQ
12 Orchard Street
SWANSEA
SA1 5AZ
Tel. 01792-642044
Fax 01792-645237

SWINDON

David Allen
Central Library
Regent Circus
SWINDON
SN1 1QG
Tel. 01793-463230
Fax 01793-541319

TAMESIDE

George Maddock
Council Offices
Wellington Road
ASHTON U LYNE
OL6 6DL
Tel. 0161-342 2035
Fax 0161-343 1732

TORFAEN

Gareth Huw Evans
Torfaen Library HQ
County Hall
PONTYPOOL
NP44 2XL
Tel. 01633-867584
Fax 01633-838609
tag97@dial.pipex.com

TOWER HAMLETS

John Hagerty
Bancroft Library
277 Bancroft Road
TOWER HAMLETS
E1 4DQ
Tel. 0171-364 2517 (2552)
Fax 0171-364 2502

TRAFFORD

Martin Gan
Trafford Town Hall
Talbot Road
STRETFORD
M32 0YZ
Tel. 0161-912 3005
Fax 0161-912 3019

UPPER NORWOOD

Christopher Dobb
Upper Norwood Lib
Westow Hill
LONDON
SE19 1TJ
Tel. 0181-670 2551
Fax 0181-670 5468

VALE OF GLAMORGAN

Christopher Edwards
Barry Library
King Square
BARRY
CF63 4RW
Tel. 01446-740688
Fax 01446-740688

WAKEFIELD

Simon Rice
Library Headquarters
Balne Lane
WAKEFIELD
WF2 0DQ
Tel. 01924-302214
Fax 01924-302245
simon rice
@GE02.POPTEL.ORG.UK

WALSALL

Ian Everall
Department of Libraries
Darwall Street
WALSALL
WS1 1TZ
Tel. 01922-653130
Fax 01922-722687
ieverall@walsplsm.demon.co.uk

WALTHAM FOREST

Colin Richardson
Central Library
High Street
LONDON
E17 7JN
Tel. 0181-520 5822

WANDSWORTH

Jane Allen
Room 223, Town Hall
High Street
WANDSWORTH
SW11
Tel. 0181-871 7753
Fax 0181-871 7753

WARWICKSHIRE

Mike Henry
Libraries and Heritage
Barrack Street
WARWICK
CV34 4TH
Tel. 01926-412166
Fax 01926-412165
warcolib@dial.pipex.com

WEST DUMBARTON

M C Taylor
Levenford House
Helenslee Road
DUMBARTON
G82 4AH
Tel. 01389-738325
Fax 01389-734204

WEST LOTHIAN

George Kerr
Library HQ
Marjoribanks Street
BATHGATE
EH48 1AN
Tel. 01506-776325
Fax 01506-776345
gkerr@libhq.demon.co.uk

WEST SUSSEX

Alan Pyant
Library Sevice Admin Centre
Tower Street
CHICHESTER
PO19 1QJ
Tel. 01243-756703
Fax 01243-756714

WESTERN ISLES

R M Eaves
Public Library
Keith Street
STORNOWAY
HS1 2QG
Tel. 01851-703064
Fax 01857-705657

WESTMINSTER

Andrew Stevens
Education & Leisure Department
Westminster City Hall
LONDON
SW1
Tel. 0171-641 3347
Fax 0171-641 3406
a.stevens@dial.pipex.com

WIGAN

Jerry Tracey
Trencherfield Mill
Wallgate
WIGAN
WN3 4EF
Tel. 01942-828187
Fax 01942-828039
j.tracey@wiganmbc.gov.uk

WILTSHIRE

Pauline Dyer
Wiltshire Council
Bythsea Road
TROWBRIDGE
BA14 8BS
Tel. 01225-713700
Fax 01225-713993

WIRRAL

J C W Norton
Westminster House
Hamilton Street
WIRRAL
L41 5FN
Tel. 0151-653 4700
Fax 0151-653 74320

WOLVERHAMPTON

Robert Johnson
Central Library
Snow Hill
WOLVERHAMPTON
WV1 3AX
Tel. 01902-312025
Fax 01902-714579

WREXHAM

Bryn Jones
Libraries and Culture
Hill Street
WREXHAM
LL1 2SN
Tel. 01978-297442
Fax 01978-297422

YORK LIBRARIES

Janet Thompson
York Library
18 Back Swinegate
YORK
Y01 2AD
Tel. 01904-552808
Fax 01904-611025

Appendix 1.1 Automated circulation

System	Authority	Total service points	Total automated	Total in realtime
ACCLAIM	N. Ireland South Eastern	26	12	12
	N. Ireland Southern	23	8	8
	N. Ireland Western	16	2	2
ALS	Buckinghamshire	34	34	34
	East Riding of Yorkshire	26	10	10
	Hertfordshire	54	53	53
	Kingston upon Hull	17	11	11
	Milton Keynes	8	8	8
	North East Lincolnshire	11	9	9
	North Lincolnshire	16	5	5
	Rotherham	15	11	6
	South Tyneside	8	7	7
ALS SYSTEM 88	Bradford	31	13	13
	Cheshire	56	44	44
	Oldham	14	14	14
	South Ayrshire	15	13	13
BLCMP	Haringey	9	9	9
	N. Ireland North Eastern	36	3	3
	Wolverhampton	21	21	21
BLCMP BLS	Bath and North East Somerset	8	3	3
	Bristol	26	8	8
	City of London	6	6	6
	Gloucestershire	39	39	39
	Liverpool	26	26	26
	North Somerset	12	2	2
	South Gloucestershire	12	2	2
	Wirral	25	7	7
BLCMP TALIS	Aberdeenshire	36	6	6
	Anglesey	10	6	6
	Bolton	15	5	5
	Conwy	13	11	11
	Cornwall	33	32	32
	Coventry	13	12	12
	East Renfrew	12	2	2
	Gwynedd	19	10	10
	Hereford and Worcester	32	32	32
	Highland	41	9	9
	Islington	11	11	11
	Kingston upon Thames	6	6	6
	Lambeth	12	10	10
	Leeds	57	18	18
	Leicester	22	12	12
	Leicestershire	52	17	17
	Northamptonshire	36	34	34
	Rutland	6	1	1
	Solihull	12	12	12
	Southwark	18	15	15
	Stockton	14	12	12
BOOK PLUS	Edinburgh	24	24	24
	Nottinghamshire	80	47	47
BOOKSHELF	Dumfries and Galloway	25	25	10
	East Lothian	12		

System	Authority	Total service points	Total automated	Total in realtime
BOOKSHELF	Orkney	9	9	9
	Perth and Kinross	13	13	13
	Renfrewshire	22	21	21
	Sandwell	19	19	19
	Scottish Borders	13	0	0
BOOKSHELF +inhouse	Wigan	16	3	3
DOBIS/LIBIS	Blaenau Gwent	7	7	7
	Caerphilly	19	19	19
	Monmouthshire	9	7	7
DS GALAXY	Aberdeen	18	18	18
	Denbighshire	8	4	4
	Devon	80	36	34
	Durham	39	5	5
	Flintshire	21	7	7
	Glasgow	32	32	32
	Kent	128	38	38
	Merton	9	9	9
	Newcastle upon Tyne	22	22	22
	Richmond	13	12	12
	Shropshire	33	24	24
	Stockport	18	18	18
	Suffolk	41	41	41
	Tower Hamlets	12	12	12
	Wandsworth	12	12	12
	West Sussex	35	35	35
	Wrexham	12	1	1
DS GALAXY 2000	Bedfordshire	26	26	26
	Birmingham	40	39	39
	Darlington	2	2	2
	Dudley	18	18	18
	Dundee	14	14	14
	Ealing	12	12	12
	Enfield	15	15	15
	Falkirk	7	7	7
	Hampshire	53	33	33
	Luton	8	8	7
	Manchester	24	24	24
	Portsmouth	9	5	5
	Sefton	13	13	13
	Southampton	11	5	5
	Surrey	53	53	53
	Walsall	20	20	20
	South Lanarkshire	25	21	21
DS MODULE 3+	N. Ireland Belfast	23	23	23
DS/GENESIS	Fife	58	10	10
DYNIX	Angus	9	9	9
	Barking and Dagenham	11	11	11
	Barnsley	23	4	4
	Berkshire	34	34	34
	Bexley	14	14	14
	Cambridgeshire	49	40	40
	East Dumbartonshire	8	8	8
	Greenwich	13	13	13
	Hackney	7	7	7
	Harrow	11	5	5
	Kensington and Chelsea	7	7	7
	Knowsley	8	6	6
	Lewisham	12	12	12
	Newham	9	9	9
	Sheffield	36	36	36
	St Helens	14	5	5
	Stirling	15	15	15
	Torfaen	4	4	4

System	Authority	Total service points	Total automated	Total in realtime
DYNIX	West Lothian	14	14	14
DYNIX Release 135	Rochdale	18	3	3
GEAC	Hillingdon	17	17	17
	Stoke on Trent	10	6	6
GEAC 9000	Barnet	17	17	17
	Bromley	15	15	15
	Camden	13	13	13
	Doncaster	38	22	22
	Essex	90	66	66
	Lancashire	40	40	40
	Norfolk	54	52	52
	Redbridge	9	9	9
	Somerset	34	23	23
GEAC 9300	Sutton	9	9	9
GEAC 9304	Westminster	12	12	12
GEAC PLUS	Bridgend	13	12	12
	Ceredigion	7	2	2
	Croydon	17	17	17
	Cumbria	53	23	23
	Hammersmith and Fulham	6	6	6
	North Tyneside	17	17	17
	Staffordshire	43	18	18
	Tameside	16	12	12
	Warwickshire	33	33	33
GENESIS	Carmarthenshire	64	17	17
	Havering	10	10	10
	Hounslow	11	11	11
	Newport	10	10	10
	North Yorkshire	45	15	15
	Oxfordshire	43	14	14
	Pembrokeshire	14	3	3
	York Libraries	15	8	8
HERITAGE	Upper Norwood	1	1	1
In-house	Bournemouth	12	9	9
	Bury	11	3	3
	Derby	11	5	5
	Derbyshire	46	13	13
	Dorset	34	23	23
	Gateshead	18	19	0
	Hartlepool	7	3	3
	Middlesbrough	13	9	9
	Northumberland	35	0	0
	Poole	10	9	9
	Redcar and Cleveland	18	7	7
	Shetland Islands	1		
	Sunderland	20	5	5
	Trafford	14	0	0
	Wakefield	29	7	7
LIBRIS Catalyst	Powys	18		
MDIS URICA	Brent	12	12	12
	Brighton and Hove	14	14	14
	Cardiff	20	17	17
	East Sussex	30		
	Kirklees	27	21	21
	Lincolnshire	54	23	23
	Moray	20	5	5
	Swindon	16	8	8
	Vale of Glamorgan	9	5	5
	Waltham Forest	12	12	12
	Wiltshire	31	26	26
OLIB	Isle of Wight	11	2	2
	Neath and Port Talbot	19		
	Swansea	20	5	3

System	Authority	Total service points	Total automated	Total in realtime
OLIB/GEAC +	Rhondda	30	24	24
SB ELECTRONICS TELEPEN 5	Calderdale	27	1	0
SIRSI UNICORN/BOOKSHELF	East Ayrshire	24	0	0

Appendix 1.2
Shared systems

Anglesey	Gwynedd, Conwy
Bath and North East Somerset	S. Gloucestershire, Bristol, N. Somerset
Bedfordshire	Luton
Bexley	Rose Bruford College
Blaenau Gwent	Monmouthshire, Torfaen. Caerphilly
Bournmouth	Poole
Bridgend	Rhondda
Brighton and Hove	East Sussex
Bristol	South Glos, N. Somerset, Bath and N.E. Somerset
Buckinghamshire	Milton Keynes
Caerphilly	Blaenau Gwent
Conwy	Gwynedd, Isle of Anglesey
Croydon	Croydon College; Schools Advisory Service
Denbighshire	Flintshire, Wrexham
Derby	Derbyshire
Derbyshire	Derby
Dorset	Bournemouth, Poole
East Riding of Yorkshire	Kingston U Hull, N.E. & N. Lincolnshire
East Sussex	Brighton & Hove
Flintshire	Denbigshire, Wrexham
Gwynedd	Conwy, Isle of Anglesey
Hampshire	Southampton, Portsmouth
Hartlepool	Redcar, Middlesborough
Highland	Highland school libraries
Hillingdon	Uxbridge college, Hillingdon hospital
Kingston upon Hull	East Riding, N.E. and N. Lincolnshire
Lancashire	Prisons, Myerscough college, Probation service
Leicester	Leicestershire
Leicestershire	Leicester, Rutland
Luton	Bedfordshire
Middlesbrough	Hartlepool, Redcar
Milton Keynes	Buckinghamshire
Monmouthshire	Blaenau Gwent, Caerphilly
N.Ireland South Eastern	N.I. Western, N.I. Southern
N.Ireland Southern	N.I. South- Eastern, N.I. Western
N.Ireland Western	N.I. Southern, N.I. Southern Eastern
North East Lincolnshire	Hull, East Riding, N. Lincolnshire
North Lincolnshire	Kingston upon Hull, N.E. Lincs, East Riding
North Somerset	S. Gloucestershire, Bristol, Bath & N.E. Somerset
Poole	Dorset, Bournemouth
Portsmouth	Hampshire till Autumn 1997
Redcar and Cleveland	Hartlepool, Middlesborough
Rutland	Leicestershire
Sandwell	Sandwell college
Somerset	Shepton Mallet prison
South Gloucestershire	Bristol, Bath and N.E. Somerset, North Glos
Southampton	Hampshire, Portsmouth
Swindon	Wiltshire
Wiltshire	Swindon
Wrexham	Denbighshire, Flintshire

Appendix 1.3
Catalogue production

	Integrated with LMS	Council mainframe	External agency
Aberdeen	YES		
Aberdeenshire	YES		
Anglesey	YES		
Barking and Dagenham	YES		
Barnet	YES		
Barnsley	YES		YES
Bath and North East Somerset	YES		
Bedfordshire	YES		
Berkshire	YES		
Bexley	YES		
Birmingham	YES		
Blaenau Gwent	YES		
Bolton	YES		
Bournemouth	YES		YES
Bradford	YES		
Brent	YES		
Bridgend	YES		YES
Brighton and Hove	YES	YES	YES
Bristol	YES		
Bromley	YES		
Buckinghamshire	YES		
Bury	YES	YES	
Caerphilly	YES		
Calderdale		YES	
Cambridgeshire	YES		
Camden	YES		
Cardiff	YES		
Carmarthenshire	YES		
Ceredigion	YES		
Cheshire	YES		
City of London	YES		
Conwy	YES		
Cornwall	YES		
Coventry	YES		
Croydon	YES		YES
Cumbria	YES		
Darlington	YES		
Denbighshire	YES		
Derby	YES	YES	
Derbyshire	YES	YES	
Devon	YES		
Doncaster	YES		
Dorset	YES	YES	
Dudley	YES		
Dumfries and Galloway	YES		
Dundee	YES		
Durham		YES	
Ealing	YES		
East Ayreshire	YES		
East Dumbartonshire	YES		
East Lothian			YES
East Renfrew	YES		

	Integrated with LMS	Council mainframe	External agency
East Riding of Yorkshire	YES		
East Sussex	YES		
Edinburgh	YES		
Enfield	YES		
Essex	YES		
Falkirk	YES		
Fife	YES		YES
Flintshire	YES		
Gateshead	YES	YES	
Glasgow	YES		
Gloucestershire	YES		
Greenwich	YES		
Gwynedd	YES		
Hackney	YES		
Hammersmith and Fulham	YES		
Hampshire		YES	
Haringey	YES		
Harrow	YES		
Hartlepool	YES	YES	
Havering	YES		
Hereford and Worcester	YES		
Hertfordshire	YES		YES
Hillingdon	YES		
Hounslow	YES		
Isle of Wight	YES		
Islington	YES		
Kensington and Chelsea	YES		
Kent	YES		
Kingston upon Hull	YES		
Kingston upon Thames	YES		
Kirklees	YES		
Knowsley	YES		
Lambeth	YES		
Lancashire	YES		
Leeds	YES		
Leicester	YES		
Leicestershire	YES		
Lewisham	YES		
Lincolnshire	YES		
Liverpool	YES		
Luton	YES		
Manchester	YES		
Merton	YES		
Middlesbrough		YES	
Milton Keynes	YES		
Monmouthshire	YES		
Moray	YES		
N. Ireland Belfast	YES		
N. Ireland North Eastern	YES		
N. Ireland South Eastern	YES	YES	
N. Ireland Southern	YES		
N. Ireland Western	YES		
Neath and Port Talbot			YES
Newcastle upon Tyne	YES		
Newham	YES		
Newport	YES		
Norfolk	YES		
North East Lincolnshire	YES		
North Lincolnshire	YES		
North Somerset	YES		
North Tyneside		YES	YES
North Yorkshire	YES		
Northamptonshire	YES		
Northumberland		YES	

	Integrated with LMS	Council mainframe	External agency
Nottinghamshire	YES		
Oldham	YES		
Orkney	YES		
Oxfordshire	YES		
Pembrokeshire	YES		
Perth and Kinross	YES	YES	
Poole	YES	YES	
Redbridge	YES		
Redcar and Cleveland		YES	YES
Renfrewshire	YES		
Rhondda	YES		
Richmond	YES		
Rochdale	YES		
Rotherham	YES		
Rutland	YES		
Sandwell	YES		
Scottish Borders			
Sefton	YES		
Sheffield	YES		
Shetland Islands	YES		
Shropshire		YES	
Solihull	YES		YES
Somerset	YES		
South Ayrshire	YES		
South Gloucestershire			YES
South Lanarkshire	YES		
South Tyneside	YES		
Southampton		YES	YES
Southwark	YES		
St Helens	YES		
Staffordshire	YES		
Stirling	YES		
Stockport	YES		
Stockton	YES		
Stoke on Trent	YES	YES	
Suffolk	YES		
Sunderland	YES	YES	
Surrey	YES		
Sutton	YES		
Swansea	YES		
Swindon	YES		
Tameside	YES		
Torfaen	YES	YES	
Tower Hamlets	YES		
Trafford	YES	YES	
Upper Norwood	YES		
Vale of Glamorgan	YES		
Wakefield	YES	YES	
Walsall	YES		
Waltham Forest	YES		
Wandsworth	YES		
Warwickshire	YES		
West Lothian	YES		
West Sussex	YES	YES	
Westminster	YES		
Wigan		YES	
Wiltshire	YES		
Wirral	YES		
Wolverhampton	YES		
Wrexham	YES		
York Libraries	YES		

Appendix 1.4
Catalogue format/access

	Online staff & public	Online staff only	Fiche/film 112	Hardcopy 113	Other 114	Libraries with OPAC access	Total OPAC terminals
Aberdeen	YES					1	7
Aberdeenshire		YES			PC-based	36	36
Anglesey	YES					6	4
Angus	YES					7	7
Barking and Dagenham	YES					11	20
Barnet	YES					17	50
Barnsley	YES		YES			4	1
Bath and NE Somerset	YES		YES			2	7
Bedfordshire		YES	YES				
Berkshire	YES					32	74
Bexley	YES					13	24
Birmingham	YES					40	238
Blaenau Gwent	YES					3	3
Bolton	YES					5	21
Bournemouth		YES	YES				
Bradford	YES					16	30
Brent	YES					12	20
Bridgend	YES					7	9
Brighton and Hove		YES			CD-ROM	14	26
Bristol	YES		YES			10	18
Bromley	YES					15	55
Buckinghamshire	YES					16	16
Bury		YES		YES		3	
Caerphilly	YES					4	4
Calderdale			YES			0	0
Cambridgeshire	YES					15	27
Camden	YES					13	24
Cardiff	YES					17	30
Carmarthenshire	YES			YES		17	64
Ceredigion			YES			0	0
Cheshire	YES					27	43
City of London	YES					6	53
Conwy	YES					11	6
Cornwall	YES					33	40
Coventry	YES					12	18
Croydon	YES					17	57
Cumbria	YES					12	15
Darlington	YES					2	
Denbighshire	YES		YES			0	0
Derby		YES	YES				
Derbyshire		YES	YES				
Devon	YES		YES	YES		2	4
Doncaster	YES					21	28
Dorset		YES	YES	YES			
Dudley	YES					7	9
Dumfries and Galloway		YES			PC-based	25	36
Dundee	YES					14	19
Durham		YES					
Ealing	YES					12	15
East Ayrshire		YES		YES		20	0

	Online staff & public	Online staff only	Fiche/film 112	Hardcopy 113	Other 114	Libraries with OPAC access	Total OPAC terminals
East Dumbartonshire	YES					8	12
East Lothian		YES	YES				
East Renfrew	YES			YES		2	12
East Riding of Yorkshire	YES					5	8
East Sussex		YES			CD-ROM		50
Edinburgh	YES					21	43
Enfield	YES					14	25
Essex	YES					66	
Falkirk	YES					7	18
Fife		YES	YES		PC-based	12	14
Flintshire		YES	YES	YES			
Gateshead		YES			CD-ROM	3	2
Glasgow	YES		YES			6	22
Gloucestershire	YES			YES		39	12
Greenwich	YES					13	27
Gwynedd	YES					8	8
Hackney	YES					4	9
Hammersmith and Fulham	YES					4	5
Hampshire			YES				
Haringey	YES					9	20
Harrow	YES		YES	YES		5	12
Hartlepool		YES	YES				
Havering	YES					1	1
Hereford and Worcester	YES					32	70
Hertfordshire	YES					53	68
Highland	YES					21	18
Hillingdon	YES					17	33
Hounslow	YES					11	19
Isle of Wight	YES		YES			3	3
Islington	YES					11	27
Kensington and Chelsea	YES					6	18
Kent	YES		YES	YES		1	2
Kingston upon Hull	YES					1	2
Kingston upon Thames	YES						21
Kirklees	YES					1	4
Knowsley	YES					7	9
Lambeth	YES					10	23
Lancashire	YES		YES			22	30
Leeds	YES					21	37
Leicester	YES					11	8
Leicestershire	YES					23	34
Lewisham	YES					12	38
Lincolnshire	YES					30	35
Liverpool	YES					26	11
Luton		YES	YES	YES			
Manchester	YES			YES		24	70
Merton	YES					9	29
Middlesbrough		YES				0	0
Midlothian		YES				1	
Milton Keynes	YES					4	7
Monmouthshire	YES					5	5
Moray	YES					1	4
N. Ireland Belfast	YES					2	9
N. Ireland North Eastern	YES		YES			5	9
N. Ireland South Eastern		YES			CD-ROM	14	14
N. Ireland Southern		YES					23
N. Ireland Western		YES				3	
Neath and Port Talbot			YES	YES			
Newcastle upon Tyne	YES			YES		22	32
Newham	YES					9	19
Newport	YES					10	15

	Online staff & public	Online staff only	Fiche/film 112	Hardcopy 113	Other 114	Libraries with OPAC access	Total OPAC terminals
Norfolk	YES					54	64
North East Lincolnshire	YES					2	3
North Lincolnshire	YES					3	6
North Somerset	YES		YES			2	3
North Tyneside		YES	YES			0	0
North Yorkshire		YES				12	22
Northamptonshire	YES					34	50
Nottinghamshire		YES				26	66
Oldham	YES					7	9
Orkney	YES					2	5
Oxfordshire		YES	YES				
Pembrokeshire		YES				0	0
Perth and Kinross	YES					5	10
Poole		YES	YES				
Portsmouth	YES					9	
Powys	YES					18	
Redbridge	YES					9	25
Redcar and Cleveland		YES	YES			11	3
Renfrewshire		YES				0	0
Rhondda	YES					7	7
Richmond	YES					13	17
Rochdale	YES		YES			1	1
Rotherham	YES					10	11
Rutland	YES					2	
Sandwell	YES					19	20
Sefton	YES					13	
Sheffield	YES					5	10
Shetland Islands	YES						19
Shropshire	YES		YES			3	3
Solihull		YES				12	19
Somerset	YES		YES			23	37
South Ayrshire	YES					13	17
South Gloucestershire	YES		YES			2	1
South Lanarkshire	YES					11	11
South Tyneside	YES					7	13
Southampton		YES	YES				
Southwark	YES					18	27
St Helens	YES					5	12
Staffordshire		YES	YES			25	0
Stirling	YES					15	20
Stockport	YES					9	25
Stockton		YES	YES			12	10
Stoke on Trent		YES	YES			7	0
Suffolk	YES					41	133
Sunderland	YES		YES			5	11
Surrey	YES					53	112
Sutton	YES					8	10
Swansea		YES	YES			0	0
Swindon	YES		YES			1	1
Tameside	YES					12	14
Torfaen	YES					2	4
Tower Hamlets	YES					7	7
Trafford	YES		YES			14	48
Upper Norwood	YES						4
Vale of Glamorgan	YES					5	8
Wakefield	YES		YES			13	6
Walsall		YES					
Waltham Forest	YES					12	26
Wandsworth	YES					12	70
Warwickshire	YES					15	30
West Lothian	YES					13	16

	Online staff & public	Online staff only	Fiche/film 112	Hardcopy 113	Other 114	Libraries with OPAC access	Total OPAC terminals
West Sussex	YES			YES		35	41
Westminster	YES					14	47
Wigan	YES					2	3
Wiltshire	YES		YES	YES		2	2
Wirral	YES		YES			23	6
Wolverhampton	YES					12	17
Wrexham		YES	YES				
York Libraries		YES					
						1939	3366

Appendix 1.5
Automated acquisitions

	Integrated with LMS	Inhouse on PC	Council mainframe	Using EDI? 120
Aberdeenshire	YES			
Anglesey	YES			YES
Angus	YES			
Barking and Dagenham	YES			
Barnet	YES			
Barnsley	YES			
Bedfordshire	YES			
Berkshire	YES			
Birmingham	YES			
Blaenau Gwent	YES			
Bolton	YES			
Bournemouth	YES			YES
Bradford	YES			
Brent	YES			
Brighton and Hove	YES			
Bromley	YES			
Buckinghamshire	YES			YES
Bury		YES		
Cambridgeshire	YES			
Camden	YES			YES
Cardiff	YES			
Carmarthenshire	YES			
Ceredigion	YES			
Cheshire			YES	
City of London	YES			YES
Conwy	YES			YES
Cornwall	YES			YES
Coventry	YES			
Croydon		YES		YES
Cumbria	YES			
Denbighshire	YES			YES
Derby	YES			YES
Derbyshire	YES			YES
Doncaster	YES			
Dorset	YES			
Dudley	YES			
Dumfries and Galloway	YES			
Dundee	YES			
Durham		YES		
Ealing	YES			
East Ayrshire	YES			YES
East Dumbartonshire	YES			YES
East Lothian	YES			
East Renfrew	YES			
East Riding of Yorkshire	YES			YES
East Sussex	YES			
Enfield	YES			
Essex	YES			YES
Falkirk	YES			YES
Fife	YES			
Flintshire	YES			YES

	Integrated with LMS	Inhouse on PC	Council mainframe	Using EDI? 120
Gateshead	YES		YES	
Glasgow	YES			YES
Gloucestershire	YES			YES
Greenwich	YES			YES
Gwynedd	YES			YES
Hackney	YES			
Hampshire			YES	
Haringey	YES			
Havering	YES			
Hereford and Worcester	YES			YES
Hertfordshire	YES			YES
Highland	YES			YES
Hounslow	YES			
Isle of Wight	YES			YES
Islington	YES			YES
Kensington and Chelsea	YES			
Kent	YES			
Kingston upon Hull	YES			YES
Kingston upon Thames	YES			
Kirklees	YES			
Knowsley	YES			
Lambeth	YES			
Lancashire	YES			
Leeds	YES			
Leicester	YES			
Leicestershire	YES			YES
Lewisham	YES			
Lincolnshire	YES			
Liverpool	YES			YES
Luton	YES			
Manchester	YES			
Merthyr Tydfil		YES		
Milton Keynes	YES			YES
Moray	YES			
N. Ireland North Eastern	YES			
N. Ireland South Eastern	YES			
N. Ireland Southern	YES			
N. Ireland Western	YES			
Neath and Port Talbot	YES			
Newcastle upon Tyne	YES			
Newham	YES			YES
Newport	YES			
Norfolk	YES			YES
North East Lincolnshire	YES			
North Lincolnshire	YES			YES
North Yorkshire	YES			
Northamptonshire				YES
Northumberland	YES			
Nottinghamshire	YES			
Oldham	YES			
Oxfordshire	YES			
Perth and Kinross	YES			
Poole	YES			
Portsmouth	YES			
Redbridge	YES			YES
Renfrewshire	YES			
Rotherham	YES			
Rutland	YES			YES
Sandwell	YES			
Scottish Borders	YES			
Sefton	YES			
Sheffield	YES			

	Integrated with LMS	Inhouse on PC	Council mainframe	Using EDI? 120
Shetland Islands		YES		
Shropshire			YES	YES
Solihull	YES			
Somerset	YES			
South Lanarkshire	YES			YES
South Tyneside				
Southampton		YES		
Southwark	YES			YES
St Helens	YES			
Staffordshire	YES			
Stockport	YES			YES
Stockton	YES			
Stoke on Trent	YES			
Suffolk	YES			
Sunderland	YES			
Surrey	YES			
Sutton	YES			
Swansea	YES			
Swindon	YES			
Tameside	YES			
Tower Hamlets	YES			
Vale of Glamorgan	YES			
Wakefield	YES			
Walsall	YES			YES
Wandsworth	YES			YES
Warwickshire	YES			
West Lothian	YES			
West Sussex			YES	
Westminster	YES			YES
Wiltshire	YES			
Wolverhampton	YES			YES
Wrexham	YES			
York Libraries	YES			

Appendix 2.1 CD-ROM

	Libraries with staff use only	Libraries with public use	Printing for public use?	Are PCs stand alone?	CD-ROM for loan	Libraries with loan CD-ROMs
Aberdeen	9	9	YES			9
Aberdeenshire	1					
Anglesey	2	2	YES	YES		
Angus	5	4		YES		
Argyll and Bute	1					
Barking and Dagenham	1					
Barnet	4	3	YES		YES	2
Barnsley	9	9	YES	YES		
Bedfordshire	19	19	YES	YES	YES	2
Berkshire	36	24	YES	YES		
Bexley	2	4	YES	YES	YES	1
Birmingham	39	1		YES	YES	1
Blaenau Gwent	2	4	YES	YES	YES	1
Bolton	10	4	YES			
Bournemouth	9			YES		
Bradford	1	1	YES		YES	1
Brent	12	12	YES	YES		12
Bridgend	2	2	YES	YES		
Brighton and Hove	1	1	YES	YES		
Bristol	4	3	YES	YES		
Bromley	6	5	YES	YES		
Buckinghamshire	2	8	YES	YES		
Bury	6	6	YES	YES		
Caerphilly		4	YES	YES		
Calderdale	2	2	YES	YES		
Cambridgeshire		15	YES		YES	2
Camden	5	12	YES			
Cardiff	1	1	YES	YES		
Carmarthenshire	64	32	YES			
Ceredigion	2			YES		
Cheshire	13	5	YES	YES	YES	22
City of London	6	6	YES		YES	1
Conwy	5	2	YES	YES		
Cornwall	5	1	YES	YES		2
Coventry	2	2	YES	YES	YES	1
Croydon	8	16	YES		YES	1
Cumbria	12	12	YES	YES	YES	3
Darlington	2					
Denbighshire	6	6	YES	YES		3
Derby		1		YES		1
Derbyshire	8	5	YES	YES		
Devon	11	10	YES	YES	YES	2
Doncaster	22	21	YES	YES		
Dorset		2	YES	YES		
Dudley	3	1	YES	YES		
Dumfries and Galloway	1	2	YES		YES	1
Dundee	6	1	YES	YES		
Durham	5	5	YES	YES		
Ealing	1			YES		
East Ayrshire	3	3	YES	YES		

	Libraries with staff use only	Libraries with public use	Printing for public use?	Are PCs stand alone?	CD-ROM for loan	Libraries with loan CD-ROMs
East Dumbartonshire	2	1		YES		
East Lothian	3	2	YES	YES		
East Riding of Yorkshire	4	1	YES	YES		
East Sussex	30	30	YES	YES	YES	2
Edinburgh	7	8		YES		
Enfield	7	6	YES	YES		
Essex	16	90	YES	YES	YES	9
Falkirk	2	2	YES	YES		2
Fife	3	10	YES	YES		
Flintshire	9	9	YES	YES		
Gateshead	19	1	YES	YES		1
Glasgow	23	23	YES	YES		23
Gloucestershire	2	2	YES		YES	2
Greenwich	2			YES		
Gwynedd	4	4	YES	YES		
Hackney	7	7	YES	YES		
Hampshire	3	5	YES	YES	YES	1
Haringey	3	3	YES	YES		
Harrow	3	1	YES	YES		
Hartlepool	1	1	YES	YES		1
Havering	2	1	YES	YES		
Hereford and Worcester		8	YES	YES		
Hertfordshire	28	28	YES			
Highland	2			YES		
Hillingdon	1	2	YES	YES		
Hounslow	1			YES		
Inverclyde	1	4	YES	YES		4
Isle of Wight	1	1	YES	YES		1
Islington	5	11	YES	YES	YES	3
Kensington and Chelsea	1	6	YES	YES	YES	1
Kent	14	14	YES	YES		14
Kingston upon Hull	7	7	YES	YES		7
Kingston upon Thames	1			YES	YES	1
Kirklees	6	6	YES	YES	YES	6
Knowsley	4	5	YES	YES		8
Lambeth		10	YES	YES		
Lancashire	1	1			YES	5
Leeds	11	10	YES	YES		11
Leicester	1	8	YES	YES		
Leicestershire		11	YES	YES		
Lewisham	1	1	YES	YES		
Lincolnshire	10	9	YES	YES	YES	1
Liverpool	1	3	YES	YES	YES	1
Luton		7	YES	YES	YES	1
Manchester	24	24	YES	YES	YES	2
Merthyr Tydfil	2	2	YES	YES		
Merton	1	3	YES	YES		
Middlesbrough	1	2	YES	YES		2
Midlothian	1	1	YES	YES		
Milton Keynes		3	YES	YES	YES	3
Monmouthshire	2	4	YES	YES	YES	1
Moray	5	5	YES	YES		
N. Ireland Belfast	23	2	YES	YES		
N. Ireland North Eastern	6	1		YES		
N. Ireland South Eastern		25	YES	YES		
N. Ireland Southern	23	23	YES	YES	YES	1
N. Ireland Western	4			YES		
Neath and Port Talbot	3	3	YES	YES		3
Newcastle upon Tyne	5	14	YES			
Newham	9	9	YES			
Newport	5	5	YES	YES		5

	Libraries with staff use only	Libraries with public use	Printing for public use?	Are PCs stand alone?	CD-ROM for loan	Libraries with loan CD-ROMs
Norfolk	3	2	YES			
North Ayrshire	6	1	YES	YES		
North East Lincolnshire	2	1	YES	YES		
North Lincolnshire	1	3	YES	YES		3
North Somerset	2			YES		
North Tyneside	3	3	YES	YES		
North Yorkshire	1					
Northamptonshire	5	4	YES	YES	YES	4
Northumberland	1	1	YES			
Nottinghamshire	9	29	YES	YES		
Oldham	1	1	YES	YES	YES	1
Orkney	1					
Oxfordshire	2	2		YES	YES	1
Pembrokeshire	1	1	YES	YES		1
Perth and Kinross	1	2	YES		YES	1
Poole		1	YES	YES		
Portsmouth	1	1	YES	YES	YES	1
Redbridge	1	1	YES			
Redcar and Cleveland	1	1	YES	YES		
Renfrewshire	2	15	YES	YES	YES	2
Rhondda	4	3	YES	YES		
Richmond	3	2	YES	YES		
Rochdale	1	1		YES		
Rotherham	6	5	YES	YES	YES	1
Salford	2	2	YES	YES		2
Sandwell	2	10	YES	YES		
Scottish Borders	4		YES	YES	YES	3
Sefton	13	13	YES	YES		
Sheffield	10	9	YES	YES		
Shetland Islands	1	1	YES			
Shropshire	10	9	YES	YES		
Solihull	2	2	YES	YES		1
Somerset	4	7	YES	YES		
South Ayrshire		6	YES	YES		
South Gloucestershire		5	YES	YES		5
South Lanarkshire	3	6	YES	YES	YES	1
South Tyneside	1	1		YES		1
Southampton	1	1	YES	YES		0
Southwark	16	16	YES	YES		
St Helens		3	YES	YES		2
Staffordshire	12	9	YES	YES	YES	2
Stirling	1	2	YES	YES		
Stockport	18	1	YES			
Stockton	3	3		YES		3
Stoke on Trent	1	1	YES	YES	YES	1
Suffolk	3	21	YES	YES	YES	2
Sunderland	2	2	YES	YES	YES	2
Surrey	9	12	YES	YES	YES	4
Sutton	3	3	YES	YES		
Swansea	1	3	YES	YES		
Tameside	5	2	YES	YES		
Torfaen	4	3		YES	YES	2
Tower Hamlets	6			YES		
Trafford	2	3	YES	YES		
Upper Norwood	5	2	YES	YES		
Vale of Glamorgan	5	5	YES	YES		5
Wakefield	3	2		YES		
Walsall	1	6	YES	YES		
Waltham Forest	1	1	YES			
Wandsworth	12	12	YES	YES		
Warwickshire	4	2	YES	YES		

	Libraries with staff use only	Libraries with public use	Printing for public use?	Are PCs stand alone?	CD-ROM for loan	Libraries with loan CD-ROMs
West Dumbarton		1	YES	YES		1
West Lothian	3			YES		
West Sussex	16	1		YES	YES	1
Western Isles	2	1	YES	YES		
Westminster	12	12	YES	YES		
Wigan	3	3	YES	YES		
Wiltshire	1			YES		
Wirral	5	5	YES	YES		
Wolverhampton	5	2	YES			
Wrexham	1	1	YES	YES		1
York Libraries	1	1	YES	YES		
	1016	1066				244

Appendix 2.2
Most popular CD-ROMs

Authority	CD-ROMs
Aberdeen	Bookfind, Business Locator, Financial Times, Herald, ICC Company Factfinder, Independent, Key British Enterprises, Marquesa, Scotsman, Thomas Register of US Companies
Aberdeenshire	BNB, Bookbank, UKOP
Anglesey	DK Way Things Work, Encarta, Guardian, Kompass, Microsoft
Angus	Bookbank, Granger's Index, Guardian/Observer, Herald (Glasgow), Keesing, Music Master, Oxford Children's Encyclopedia, Scotsman, Times/Sunday Times, Who's Who
Barking and Dagenham	BNB, Bookfind
Barnet	Bookwise, Broker, ECCTIS, Guardian, Independent, Keynote, Statutory Instruments, Telegraph, Times, World Magazine Bank
Barnsley	Ask Me, BNB, Bookbank, Companies House Directory, Encarta, Encyclopaedia Britannica, Image select, Microsoft Dangerous Creatures, Stockseeker, Times
Berkshire	ASSIA, BBIP, BNB, Bookbank, Bookfind, Eurolaw/UKOP, Fame, Globus Books in Print, Ulrich's
Bexley	Ancient Lands, Art Gallery, Encarta, Financial Times, Musical Instruments, Select Phone, The Way Things Work, UKOP, World Magazine Index
Birmingham	Bookfind, Business Locator, Extel, Kompass, LISA, Standards Infodisk, Telephone Directory, UKOP
Blaenau Gwent	DK History of the World, DK Human Body, DK Nature, DK PB Bear, DK Space and Universe, DK World Atlas, Encarta, George Shrinks, Guardian, Haunted House
Bolton	Bookbank, Britannica, European Commentaries, Financial Times, Guardian 96, Guardian Jan-Mar 97, In Your Area, Mintel, Official Journal of the EC, UK Markets
Bournemouth	Companies House Directory, Mapview, Mintel, Telepower Pro, Thompsons UK, Times Newspaper, UKOP, World Magazine Bank
Bradford	Census, How Things Work, Hutchinsons Encyclopaedia, Independent, Kompass, McCarthy, Mintel
Brent	Encarta, Guardian, Hutchinsons Encyclopaedia, Independent, Times
Bridgend	BBC Wales, Britannica, Colliers Encyclopaedia, Driving Theory Test, Information Finder, Times, Western Mail
Brighton and Hove	BNB, BNI, ECCTIS, Encarta, Extel, OJCD, Palmers Index to the Times, Whitakers Books in Print
Bristol	BT Phone Disc, Census on CD-ROM, Espace Access, Financial Times, Guardian, Independent, Marquesa, McCarthy, Pro CD, Times
Bromley	Ancient Lands, Bookbank, British Newspaper Index, ECCTIS, Encarta 97, Encyclopaedia of Science, Hansard, Justis Parliament, The Way Things Work, Times
Buckinghamshire	British Newspaper Index, Britannica, BT Phone Disc, Encarta, Eurostst, Guardian/Observer 1996, Key British Enterprises, Kompass, Study Link, World Book Encylopaedia
Bury	Ancient Lands, Changing Times, Encarta 96, Eyewitness, Grolier Science Fiction, World War 2
Caerphilly	Encarta, How Things Work, Push UK, Ultimate Human Body
Calderdale	Bookbank, Bookfind, Cinemania, Encarta, Family Search, Financial Times, Guardian, Musical Instruments, Statuatory Instruments, Times
Cambridgeshire	Daily Telegraph, Encarta, Encyclopaedia of Science, Extel, Grolier Encyclopaedia, Guardian, Independent, Ultimate Human Body, Times, Times Index
Cardiff	BHI, Bookbank, Bookfind, ECCTIS, Encarta, Financial Times, Independent, McCarthy, UKOP, Which University
Ceredigion	Independent, Phone Disc, Western Mail
Cheshire	Britannica, BT phone book, Changing Times, Encarta, Encylopaedia of Nature, Financial Times, Guardian, Keesings, Oxford Childrens Encyclopaedia, Way things work
City of London	American Phone Discs, BNB, Commons Hansard, Dictionary of National Biography, F & S Plus text, Financial Times, FT McCarthy, Palmers Index to Times, Peusner

Authority	CD-ROMs
Conwy	ECCTIS, Encarta, Encyclopaedia Britannica, History, How Things Work, Nature, Ordnance Survey, The Body, Times, Which University
Cornwall	Espace, Eurolaw, Europe in the Round, Galet Quotations, Keynoted, Mintel, Oxford English Dictionary, USA Phone Fiche, World Book Encyclopaedia
Coventry	3D ATLAS, Guiness Disk of Records, Hutchinson Encyclopaedia, Mavis Beacon Typing Tutor, McGraw Hill Encyclopaedia, Microsoft Art Gallery, Encarta, Professor Multimedia, Push CD (Guide to Universities), Think and Talk Italian, Think and Talk Spanish, Think and Talk French, Think and Talk German
Croydon	Companies House, Ecctis, Encarta, Guardian, Independent, Kompass UK, Maps, McCarthy, Minitel, Times
Cumbria	BNB, Bookbank, Bookdata, Britannica, Encarta, Guardian
Denbighshire	DK Encyclopaedia of Nature, DK Encyclopaedia of Science, DK History of the World, DK The Way Things Work, DK Ultimate Human Body, Encarta, Independent, Macmillan Dictionary for Children, My First Incredible Amazing Dictionary, The Times and Sunday Times
Derby	Daily Telegraph, Guardian, Independent, Social Trends, Times
Devon	Changing Times, Global Book Bank, Glover News Index, Guardian, Investigating 20th century art, Microsoft Art Gallery, PUSH CD, UKOP, World Book, World Reference Atlas
Doncaster	Encyclopaedia Britannica, Cinemania, Creative Writer, Encyclopaedia of Science, Encarta, Exploring Earth Science, Fine Artist, Hutchinsons Encylopaedia, Oxford Children's Encyclopaedia, Ultimate Human Body
Dudley	Bookbank, Britannica, Economist, Guardian, Rail Journey Planner, Times, Which School, Which University
Dumfries and Galloway	Encyclopaedia Britannica, Bookbank
Dundee	Census, Espace Access, KBE 200, Medline, Selectphone, Thomas Register
Durham	Encarta, Northern Echo, Times, Toolworks
Ealing	Bibliographic
East Lothian	Arthur's Birthday, Bookbank, Britannica, Children's encyclopaedia., DNB, HOBS, Encarta, Transport Tycoon, Who's Who
East Sussex	BABS, BLGC, BNB, Bookbank, Encarta, Music Master, World Book Bank
Edinburgh	BT Phone Disc, Ecctis, Encyclopaedias, Extel, Guardian, Independent, McCarthy, Scotsman, Times, Training Access Point
Enfield	Business Locator, Economist, Family Search, Financial Times, Guardian, Independent, Key British Enterprises, New Scientist, Telegraph, Times
Essex	Bookbank, BT Phone Disc, Dun & Bradstreet Business Locator, Economist, Independent, Keynote, LIFE, One Source Company Info
Falkirk	Britannica, Computers Don't Bite, Egon Ronay, Grolier, Key British Enterprises, Scotsman, The Herald, Times, Which School, World Book
Fife	Atlas, Bookbank, Compton's, Dangerous Creatures, Guardian, Human Body, Incredible Amazing Dictionary, Scotsman
Gateshead	Britannica, Current Technology Index, EC Infodisc, Encarta 97, Film Index International, Financial Times, Guardian, Newcastle Evening Chronicle, Statutory Instruments, Times
Glasgow	Autoroute Express, BHI, British Newspaper Index, Fame, Family Search, Marquesa, McCarthy, Mediline, UK Official Publications
Gloucestershire	BNI, Encarta, Encyclopaedia of Nature, Guiness Book of Records, History of the World, Hutchinson Encyclopaedia, IT on CD, PB Bears Picnic, Where's Wally at the Circus, World Atlas
Greenwich	Bookbank, Bookfind, British Newspaper Index, Census, Guardian Index, Laser, Lisa Plus, RED, Times
Hampshire	Bookbank, Economist, Encarta, Financial Times, Guardian, Independent, Standards Infodisc, Statutory Instruments, Times and Sunday Times, UKOP
Harrow	Bookbank, Encarta
Havering	BNB, Bookbank, Celex, Guardian, Statutory Instruments
Hereford and Worcester	Britannica, Guardian, Times
Hertfordshire	BHI, BNB, Bookbank, Eurocat, Eurolaw, Infodisc, KBE, UKOP
Highland	BIP+, BL CAT, BNB, Bookbank, BOP+, RED, UKOP
Hillingdon	BNB, Bookbank, Colliers Encyclopaedia , Daily Telegraph, ECCTIS, Encarta, Europe in the Round, Guardian, Independent, UKOP
Hounslow	BM Cat, BNB, Bookbank

Authority	CD-ROMs
Inverclyde	Britannica, Encarta, Glasgow Herald
Islington	Encarta
Kent	British Newspaper Index, Financial Times, General Academic Index, Times, World Book
Kingston upon Thames	BBIP, BNB
Kirklees	Ancient Lands, Dinosaurs, DK Birds, Encarta, Encyclopaedia of Nature, History of the World, Human Body, Musical Instruments, Space Encyclopaedia, The Way Things Work
Knowsley	Ancient Lands, Art Gallery, Creative Writer, Encarta, Encyclopaedia of Nature, Encyclopaedia of Science, Encyclopaedia of World History, Grolier Encyclopaedia, Human Body, Musical Instruments
Lancashire	Bookfind, Books OP, Guardian, Library of Congress, Premium, Times
Leeds	British Newspaper Index, Business Source Plus, D & B Business Locator, Encarta, FT Prices, Information Access, KBE 200, Marquesa, McCarthy, UKOP
Leicester	BHI, Encarta, Family Search, Financial Times, General Academic Index, Guardian, Snapshots, Social Trends, Daily Telegraph, Times
Leicestershire	Cinemania, Encarta, Guardian, History of the World, How Things Work, Independent, Musical Instruments, Oxford Children's Encyclopaedia, Times/SundayTimes, World Book
Lincolnshire	BNB, DK Nature, DK Science, Encarta, Global Bookbank, Hutchinson Encyclopaedia, Independent, Key British Enterprises
Liverpool	Bookbank, CTI, Extel, Kompass UK, Patent, UKOP
Luton	Business & Industry, Companies House, Encarta, Encyclopaedia of Nature, Eurolaw, Financial Times, Great Artists, Guardian, Human Body, Keynotes
Manchester	BNB, Bookbank, BHI, EECTIS, Financial Times, Guardian, Independent, Telegraph, Times, UKOP
Merton	Encarta 96, Harry in the Haunted House, Magic School Bus in the Human Body, Magic School Bus in the Solar System, Magic School Bus Under the Ocean, Sammy's Science House, Topsy and Tim at School, Topsy and Tim at Granny and Grampa's, Topsy and Tim at the Supermarket, Tortoise and the Hare
Middlesbrough	British Standards, Encarta, Extel, Financial Times, Guardian, How Things Work, Independent, New Scientist, Northern Echo, Times
Milton Keynes	Britannica, Encarta
Monmouthshire	25 Years social trends, Cinemania, Dinosaurs, ECCTIS, Encarta, Guardian, Kompass, PB Bear, PUSH CD, Western Mail
N. Ireland Belfast	BHI, BNB, Bookfind, Fame, Global Books in Print, Guardian, McCarthy, Prophone, RED, UKOP
N. Ireland Western	BCCCS-Acclaim, Bookfind, Whitakers Bookbank
Neath and Port Talbot	Castle Explorer, Chronicle of the 20th Century, Encarta, Eyewitness History of the World, Hutchinsons Multimedia Encyclopedia, Interactive Atlas of Great Britain, Microsoft Art Gallery, Stowaway, The Way Things Work, World Book Encyclopedia
Newcastle upon Tyne	Bibliographic Tools, BNB, BT Phone Disc, Encarta, Guardian, Independent, Key British Enterprises, McCarthy, Northern Echo
Newham	Ancient Lands, Dinosaurs, Encarta, Fish Who Could Wish, Human Body, Musical Instruments, Oxford Childrens Encylopaedia, Way Things Work, World, World Atlas
Newport	Ask Me, Bookbank, Encarta 97, Encarta World Atlas 97, Financial Times, Guardian, Oscar, TC Farries Database, Times / Sunday Times
Norfolk	Ft McCarthy, Independent, KBE 200,000, Keynote Market Research, New Scientist, SI-CD, Times and Sunday Times, UK Business Locator, Who Owns Whom Worldwide, World Magazine Bank
North East Lincolnshire	Autoroute express, BNB, BSI, Census Data, Chapter and Verse, Companies House Directory, Encarta, Europe in the Round, UK Markets, UKOP
North Lincolnshire	British Standards, Census 1991, Dictionary of National Biography, Digital Mapping, Encarta, Facts about Britain, Financial Times, Funder Finder, Social Trends 1970-95, The Guardian
North Somerset	Encarta, Phone Disc, Times/Sunday Times
Northamptonshire	1991 Census, Ancient Lands, Arthur's Teacher Trouble, British Standards, Encarta, Financial Times, Independent, Kompass Uk, Single Market, World Reference Atlas
Northumberland	Bookbank, Encarta, English Poetry, Grangers Poetry, Guardian, Newcastle Journal, UKOP, World of Poetry
Nottinghamshire	Bookbank, BHI, BT Phone Disc, DK History, Encarta, Hutchinson Encyclopaedia, McCarthy, The Way Things Work, Times 1996, US Phonedisc
Oldham	Britannica, CCH Business Profile, Citizens Charter, ECTIS, Guardian

Authority	CD-ROMs
Oxfordshire	Bookfind, Encarta, EU Info Disc, Eurolaw, Eyewitness, Key British Enterprises, Keynote, Microsoft Art Gallery, Oscar, ROM READ
Pembrokeshire	BNB, Bookfind, Cinemania, Family Search
Perth and Kinross	BNB, Bookbank, Bookfind, Bowker, British Library Catalogue, Global Books in Print, Guardian, Times, UKOP, World Magazine Bank
Poole	Eurolaw, Financial Times, Guardian, Independent, Key British Enterprises, Mapview, Social Trends, Standards Infodisc
Portsmouth	Ecinfodisc, Economist, Eurolaw, Extel, Guardian, Patents, Phonebase, Standards Infodisc, UKOP
Redbridge	BNB, Global Books in Print, Gramophone, Kompass Europe, LISA, UKOP
Rhondda	BNB, Britannica, How it Works, Keesings, Music work, Stowaway, Times, Western Mail, Whitakers Bookbank, World Book Encyclopaedia
Richmond	Bookfind, ECCTIS PLUS, Encarta 96, Eyewitness, Guardian, Hutchinson Multimedia, New Scientist, Small Blue Planet, Viscount, Whitaker Web
Rochdale	Basic French, German and Spanish, English Basic Skills, How Computers, Mavis Beacon Teaches Typing, MS Internet Explorer Quick and Easy, Netscape Navigator Quick and Easy, Presentation Skills, Windows 95 Quick and easy
Salford	Atlas, Encyclopaedia, Environment, Guardian, OS Maps
Sandwell	Britannica, DK History of the World, DK Human Body, DK Science, DK The Way Things Work, Encarta, Europe in the Round, Justis, Keynote, Times and Sunday Times
Sefton	Encarta, Daily Mail, Ebeco World Magazine Bank, Guardian, Sunday Times, Telegraph, Times
Sheffield	Books in Print, Britannica, Current Technology Index, Espace, EXTEL, IGI, Marquesa, Newspaper Index, Sports Discus
Solihull	Chronicle of the 20th Century, DK 3D Skeleton, DK Castle Explorer, Dk History of the World, DK Human Body, DK Incredible Dictionary, DK World Reference Atlas, DL Encyclopaedia of Science, Encarta 97, Pocahontas
Somerset	Changing Times, ECCTIS, Financial Times, Global Bookbank, Guardian, Independent, KBE, Telegraph, Times, World Magazine Bank
South Lanarkshire	Encarta, How Things Work, My First Dictionary, Phone Disc, The Human Body, Typing Tutor
South Tyneside	BNI, Encyclopaedia Britannica, Colliers Encyclopaedia, Encarta, Eurolaw, Guardian, Newcastle Journal, Oxford English Dictionary, Social Trends, Times
Southampton	BHI, CTI, Economist, Extel, Financial Times, Guardian, Independent, Times
Staffordshire	Ask Me, Bookbank, Business Locator, Clover Newspaper Index, ECTIS, Eurolaw, Times and Sunday Times, UKOP
Stirling	Encyclopaedia Britannica, IGI, Times
Stockport	BNB, Bookbank, Bookfind, Extel, Financial Times, Guardian, Kompass 2000, Kompass Europe, Times, UKOP
Stockton	Encyclopaedia Britannica, Colliers Encyclopaedia, Companies House Register, Daily Telegraph, DNB, Facts About Today, Magic School Bus Explores the Solar System, Northern Echo, OED, The Haunted House
Stoke on Trent	Art Index, BHI, Current Technology Index, English Poetry Index, Eurolaw, Facts about Britain, Independent, MS Encarta, Social Trends, Times
Suffolk	Daily Telegraph, Encarta, Europe in the Round, Financial Times, Guardian, Independent, New Scientist, Phone Disc, Times, UKOP
Sunderland	Bookbank, Guardian, McCarthy
Surrey	Encarta, BNB, Bookbank, Encyclopaedia Britannica, Encyclopaedia of Science and Technology, Guardian, Observer, The Times, UKOP, World Reference Atlas
Sutton	ECCTIS, Encarta, Financial Times, Guardian, Mintel, New Scientist, Times, UKOP, Bookbank
Tameside	BNB, Bookbank, Encarta, HMSO, RED, Suppliers CD-ROM Tools
Torfaen	Encyclopaedia Britannica, BT Phone Disc, ECCTIS/PUSH, Encarta, Europages, Guardian, Human Body, Kompass, Times Newspaper, Western Mail
Tower Hamlets	BL CAT, BNB, Bookbank
Trafford	Companies House Register, Encarta, Times and Sunday Times
Walsall	MS World Atlas, DK Ultimate Human Body, Guardian, Haunted House, Key British Enterprises, MS Cinemania, Encarta, PB Bear, Times, Winnie the Witch
Waltham Forest	Bookbank, Changing Times, ECCTIS, Guardian, SASPAC 1991 Census
Wandsworth	Bookfind, BHI, Daily Telegraph, Economist, Financial Times, Guardian, Kompass, Rail Journey Planner, Times, World Magazine Bank
Warwickshire	Encyclopaedia Britannica, BT Phone Disc, Dinosaurs, Encarta, Guardian/Observer, The Times, The Way Things Work, Ultimate Human Body, World Book

Authority	CD-ROMs
West Lothian	Morley Stockseeker, Whitaker Web
West Sussex	Bookbank, RED
Western Isles	BNB, Multimedia Encyclopaedia
Westminster	Cinemania, Daily Telegraph, ECCTIS, Encarta, Guardian, Hutchinson Multimedia Encyclopaedia, Independent, Key British Enterprises, Medline, Times
Wigan	GBIP, GBOP, Whitakers Bookbank
Wiltshire	BNB, Boston Spa Serials, Bowker, Euro Law, HMSO UKOP, Whitaker
Wolverhampton	Ancient Lands, BNB, Changing Times, GBIP, Guardian, Human Body, PB Bear, Space, Times
Wrexham	Dictionary of Living World, Encarta, Grangers Index to Poetry, Thomas Register, Times, World Reference Atlas
York Libraries	Discover York, Financial Times, Infopaedia, KBE, Statutory Instruments, Telepower, World Magazine Bank

Appendix 2.3
Internet availability

	PCs with Internet access	Total PCs for public use	Total libraries connected	Libraries with public access	Total leased lines	Total dial-up	Total council network
Aberdeen	4		1			4	
Aberdeenshire	2	1	1	1		2	
Argyll and Bute	1		1				
Barnet	5		2				2
Barnsley	9	9	8	8		8	
Bath and N.E. Somerset	5	5	1	1	1		
Bedfordshire	3	1	3	1		3	
Berkshire	30	4	4	4		8	22
Bexley	2		1			2	
Birmingham	6		1	1	1	1	
Blaenau Gwent	3		2			3	
Bolton	2		1			1	
Bradford	8	4	2	2		2	1
Brent	17	17	3	3			1
Bridgend	5	5	2	2	1	1	
Brighton and Hove	2	2	2	2		1	
Bristol	4	1	2	1		8	
Bromley	3		1			1	
Bury	2		2			4	
Caerphilly	6	3	4	3		6	
Calderdale	5	1	1	1		1	
Cambridgeshire	20	13	5	5		3	1
Cardiff	2	1	1	1		2	
Carmarthenshire	1		1			1	
Cheshire	8	5	8	5		8	
City of London	1		1		1		
Conwy	5	2	5	2	1	4	
Coventry	4		2			2	
Croydon	20	6	3	3	3		
Cumbria	15	10	10	10		10	
Denbighshire	5	4	4	4		5	
Derbyshire	1		1			1	
Devon	18	1	4	1		13	5
Dorset	1					1	
Dudley	3		3				3
Dumfries and Galloway	2	1	2	1		2	
Dundee	8	7	1	1		1	7
Durham	4	3	4	3	2	2	
East Ayrshire	4	3	3	3		2	2
East Dumbartonshire							
East Lothian	3	2	2	2			
East Riding of Yorkshire	7		3			10	
East Sussex	8	2	2	2		2	
Edinburgh	3	2	2	2		2	
Enfield	6	3	3	2		3	
Essex	30	8	3	5		4	1
Falkirk	2		1			2	
Fife	1	1	1	1	1		
Flintshire	1		1			1	
Gateshead	6	1	1	1		1	1

	PCs with Internet access	Total PCs for public use	Total libraries connected	Libraries with public access	Total leased lines	Total dial-up	Total council network
Glasgow	5		1		5		
Gloucestershire	15	12	3	3			3
Gwynedd	4	0				1	
Hackney	24	18	7	7			7
Hammersmith & Fulham	2		2			2	
Hampshire	36	5	31	5		6	31
Hartlepool	1		1			1	
Hereford and Worcester	3		3			3	
Hertfordshire							
Hillingdon	1		1			1	
Hounslow	4	1	1	1		1	
Isle of Wight	2	2	2	2			
Islington	11	4	2	2			
Kensington and Chelsea	3	1	1	1	1	2	
Kent	3						
Kingston upon Hull	5		1				
Kingston upon Thames	9	1	3	1		2	1
Kirklees	4		1				
Lancashire	25	18	18	18			
Leeds	12		1	1			
Leicester	1		1			1	
Leicestershire	8	1	1	1			
Lewisham	3	2	2	2			3
Lincolnshire	2	1	2	1		2	
Liverpool	1		1			1	
Luton	2	2	1	1			
Manchester	20	5	4	4		20	
Merthyr Tydfil	1		1			1	
Middlesbrough	1		1				
Midlothian	1						
Monmouthshire	4	2	2	1		2	
Moray		2	2	2			
N. Ireland Belfast	1		1			1	
N. Ireland North Eastern	6	1	1	1		1	
N. Ireland South Eastern	5	2	4	2	5		
N. Ireland Southern	1						
N. Ireland Western	3		3		3		
Neath and Port Talbot	5	1	1	1		1	
Newcastle upon Tyne	12	2	2	2		2	
Newham	4		1				4
Newport	2	2	1	1		1	
Norfolk	40	2	2	1		2	1
North East Lincolnshire	3	3	1	1	1		
North Lincolnshire	1	1	1	1		1	
North Tyneside	1		1			1	
North Yorkshire	1					1	
Northamptonshire	2		2		2		
Northumberland	1		1				1
Nottinghamshire	11		8			9	2
Oldham	1		1				1
Oxfordshire							
Perth and Kinross	3	2	1	1		1	
Portsmouth	1		1			1	
Powys					3		15
Redcar and Cleveland	4	1	1	1			1
Renfrewshire	4	1	4	1		4	
Rhondda	1	1	1	1		1	
Richmond	1		1			1	
Rotherham	5	1	1	1			1
Sandwell	17	10	5	5		2	3
Scottish Borders	1						

	PCs with Internet access	Total PCs for public use	Total libraries connected	Libraries with public access	Total leased lines	Total dial-up	Total council network
Sheffield	8		6			6	
Shetland Islands		1		1			
Shropshire	12	10	12	10		12	
Solihull	8	6	1	1	1		
Somerset	9	5	3	2	1	2	
South Ayrshire	25	19	2	2	1	1	
South Lanarkshire	1	1	1	1		1	
South Tyneside	1		1	1	1		
Southampton		1	5	1		1	5
Southwark	4	2	2	2		2	
Staffordshire	7		2				
Stirling	2	2	2	2		2	
Stockport	2	1	1	1		2	
Suffolk	27	13	10	10			
Sunderland	3	2	2	2		2	
Surrey	20	9	10	8	2	13	2
Sutton	3		1			1	
Swansea	2	1	1	1			
Tameside	4		3				
Torfaen	3	2	2	2		2	
Tower Hamlets	1		1			1	
Trafford	3		3			3	
Wakefield	1	1	1	1			
Walsall	6	1	1	1			1
Waltham Forest	30						
Wandsworth	2	2	2	2			
Warwickshire	13	3	4	3		4	
West Lothian	3						
West Sussex	9		3			2	1
Westminster	21	2	5	2	3	2	
Wigan	4						1
Wiltshire	2		1			1	
Wirral	2	1	1	1		1	
Wolverhampton	2		1				
Wrexham	3		1			3	
York Libraries	2	1	1	1			
	908	321	357	215	40	278	130

Appendix 2.4
Internet: staff use

	Technical staff	Senior management	Reference staff	Other
Aberdeen		YES	YES	
Aberdeenshire			YES	YES
Argyll and Bute		YES	YES	YES
Barnet	YES		YES	YES
Barnsley	YES	YES	YES	YES
Bedfordshire		YES	YES	
Berkshire	YES	YES	YES	Librarians
Bexley	YES	YES	YES	
Birmingham		YES	YES	
Blaenau Gwent	YES	YES	YES	YES
Bolton	YES			YES
Bradford	YES	YES	YES	YES
Brent	YES	YES	YES	YES
Bridgend	YES	YES	YES	
Brighton and Hove				Central library staff
Bristol	YES	YES	YES	YES
Bromley	YES	YES	YES	
Bury		YES		
Caerphilly		YES	YES	YES
Calderdale		YES	YES	
Cambridgeshire	YES	YES	YES	YES
Cardiff	YES	YES	YES	YES
Carmarthenshire		YES		
Cheshire	YES	YES	YES	
City of London				YES
Conwy		YES	YES	Front line staff
Cornwall			YES	
Coventry	YES		YES	YES
Croydon	YES	YES	YES	
Cumbria	YES	YES	YES	YES
Denbighshire		YES	YES	
Derbyshire		YES		Request unit
Devon	YES	YES	YES	YES
Dorset	YES			
Dudley	YES	YES	YES	YES
Dumfries & Galloway				YES
Dundee				ALL
Durham		YES	YES	
East Ayrshire		YES	YES	YES
East Dumbartonshire	YES	YES	YES	
East Lothian				YES
East Riding	YES	YES	YES	
East Sussex	YES	YES	YES	
Edinburgh			YES	Project staff
Enfield	YES		YES	YES
Essex	YES	YES	YES	
Falkirk	YES	YES	YES	
Fife				YES
Flintshire	YES	YES	YES	
Gateshead	YES	YES	YES	YES
Glasgow		YES	YES	

	Technical staff	Senior management	Reference staff	Other
Gloucestershire	YES	YES	YES	YES
Gwynedd			YES	
Hackney	YES	YES	YES	YES
Hammersmith & Fulham			YES	
Hampshire		YES	YES	YES
Hartlepool			YES	
Hereford & Worcestershire		YES	YES	
Hertfordshire	YES	YES	YES	YES
Hillingdon	YES	YES	YES	YES
Hounslow	YES		YES	
Isle of Wight		YES	YES	YES
Islington		YES	YES	
Kensington & Chelsea			YES	YES
Kent	YES	YES		
Kingston upon Hull	YES		YES	
Kingston upon Thames	YES	YES	YES	YES
Kirklees	YES	YES	YES	
Lancashire	YES	YES	YES	
Leeds	YES	YES	YES	
Leicester			YES	
Leicestershire	YES	YES	YES	YES
Lewisham		YES	YES	
Lincolnshire				ALL
Liverpool			YES	
Luton		YES	YES	YES
Manchester	YES	YES	YES	
Merthyr Tydfil		YES	YES	
Middlesbrough			YES	
Midlothian	YES	YES	YES	YES
Monmouthshire		YES		YES
Moray				
N. Ireland Belfast		YES	YES	
N. North Eastern	YES	YES	YES	
N. Ireland South Eastern	YES	YES	YES	
N. Ireland Southern	YES	YES	YES	
N. Ireland Western		YES	YES	YES
Neath & Port Talbot		YES	YES	
Newcastle upon Tyne		YES	YES	YES
Newham	YES	YES	YES	
Newport	YES	YES	YES	YES
Norfolk	YES	YES	YES	
N.E. Lincolnshire	YES	YES	YES	ALL
North Lincolnshire		YES	YES	
North Tyneside	YES	YES	YES	YES
North Yorkshire	YES	YES	YES	
Northamptonshire	YES	YES	YES	
Northumberland	YES	YES	YES	
Nottinghamshire	YES	YES	YES	
Oldham		YES		
Oxfordshire	YES	YES	YES	
Perth and Kinross	YES	YES	YES	
Portsmouth		YES	YES	
Powys				
Redcar & Cleveland	YES	YES	YES	
Renfrewshire	YES	YES	YES	
Rhondda	YES	YES	YES	
Richmond		YES		
Rotherham		YES	YES	
Sandwell		YES	YES	
Scottish Borders	YES	YES	YES	
Sheffield		YES	YES	
Shetland Islands				

	Technical staff	Senior management	Reference staff	Other
Shropshire			YES	YES
Solihull	YES	YES	YES	YES
Somerset	YES	YES	YES	
South Ayrshire		YES	YES	YES
South Lanarkshire				
South Tyneside			YES	
Southampton	YES	YES	YES	ALL
Southwark	YES	YES	YES	
Staffordshire	YES	YES	YES	YES
Stirling				YES
Stockport	YES	YES	YES	
Suffolk	YES	YES	YES	Record Office
Sunderland	YES	YES	YES	
Surrey	YES	YES	YES	YES
Sutton	YES	YES	YES	
Swansea		YES	YES	YES
Tameside			YES	YES
Torfaen			YES	YES
Tower Hamlets			YES	
Trafford			YES	
Wakefield		YES	YES	
Walsall	YES	YES	YES	
Waltham Forest	YES	YES	YES	
Wandsworth			YES	
Warwickshire	YES	YES	YES	
West Lothian	YES	YES	YES	
West Sussex	YES	YES	YES	
Westminster	YES	YES	YES	YES
Wigan	YES			
Wiltshire	YES			
Wirral		YES	YES	
Wolverhampton		YES	YES	
Wrexham				
York Libraries			YES	YES

Appendix 2.5
Internet: types of staff use

	Reference work	Professional development	E-mail	Exploration	Online database	System support	Cataloguing/ acquisitions	Other
Aberdeenshire	YES			YES				
Argyll and Bute	YES		YES					
Barnet		YES	YES	YES		YES		
Barnsley	YES	YES	YES	YES				
Bedfordshire	YES	YES	YES	YES				
Berkshire	YES	YES	YES	YES				
Bexley	YES	YES	YES	YES	YES		YES	
Birmingham	YES	YES	YES	YES				
Blaenau Gwent	YES	YES	YES	YES	YES		YES	
Bolton	YES		YES		YES			
Bradford	YES	YES	YES	YES	YES	YES		
Brent	YES	YES	YES	YES				
Bridgend	YES	YES	YES	YES	YES			
Brighton and Hove	YES		YES	YES				
Bristol	YES	YES	YES	YES		YES		
Bromley	YES	YES	YES	YES	YES	YES		
Bury				YES				
Caerphilly	YES	YES	YES	YES				
Calderdale	YES		YES	YES				
Cambridgeshire	YES	YES	YES	YES	YES			
Cardiff	YES	YES	YES	YES		YES	YES	
Carmarthenshire				YES				
Cheshire	YES	YES	YES	YES				
City of London	YES	YES		YES				
Conwy	YES	YES	YES	YES	YES			
Cornwall	YES				YES			
Coventry	YES	YES	YES	YES	YES	YES	YES	
Croydon	YES	YES	YES	YES	YES			
Cumbria	YES		YES		YES			
Denbighshire	YES	YES	YES	YES				
Derbyshire		YES		YES				
Devon	YES	YES	YES	YES	YES	YES		
Dorset		YES		YES				
Dudley	YES	YES	YES	YES				
Dumfries and Galloway	YES	YES		YES				
Dundee	YES	YES	YES	YES	YES	YES		
Durham								
East Ayrshire	YES	YES	YES	YES	YES			
East Dumbartonshire	YES	YES				YES		
East Lothian	YES	YES	YES	YES				
East Riding	YES	YES	YES	YES	YES			
East Sussex	YES				YES	YES		
Edinburgh	YES	YES	YES	YES		YES		
Enfield	YES	YES	YES	YES	YES			
Essex	YES	YES	YES	YES	YES	YES	YES	
Falkirk	YES	YES	YES	YES	YES			
Fife				YES				
Flintshire	YES	YES	YES	YES				
Gateshead	YES	YES	YES	YES	YES	YES		
Glasgow	YES	YES	YES	YES				
Gloucestershire	YES	YES	YES	YES	YES	YES	YES	

	Reference work	Professional development	E-mail	Exploration	Online database	System support	Cataloguing/ acquisitions	Other
Gwynedd	YES				YES			
Hackney	YES	YES	YES	YES	YES			
Hammersmith and Fulham			YES	YES	YES			
Hampshire	YES	YES	YES	YES	YES	YES	YES	
Hartlepool	YES		YES	YES				
Hereford and Worcestershire	YES		YES	YES	YES			
Hertfordshire	YES	YES	YES	YES	YES	YES		
Hillingdon	YES	YES	YES	YES				
Hounslow	YES	YES	YES	YES				
Isle of Wight	YES	YES	YES	YES				
Islington	YES	YES	YES		YES			
Kensington and Chelsea	YES		YES					
Kent	YES	YES	YES	YES	YES	YES		
Kingston upon Hull	YES	YES		YES	YES			
Kingston upon Thames	YES	YES		YES	YES	YES		Training
Kirklees	YES	YES						
Lancashire	YES	YES	YES	YES	YES	YES		
Leeds	YES	YES	YES	YES		YES		
Leicester	YES	YES		YES	YES			
Leicestershire		YES	YES	YES		YES		
Lewisham	YES		YES	YES				
Lincolnshire	YES	YES	YES	YES	YES		YES	
Liverpool	YES		YES	YES	YES			
Luton	YES	YES		YES				
Manchester	YES	YES	YES	YES	YES			
Merthyr Tydfil	YES		YES					
Middlesbrough	YES	YES		YES	YES			
Midlothian	YES	YES	YES	YES	YES	YES		
Monmouthshire	YES		YES	YES	YES			
Moray	YES	YES		YES				
N. Ireland Belfast	YES		YES	YES	YES			
N. Ireland North Eastern								
N. Ireland South Eastern	YES	YES	YES	YES				
N. Ireland Southern	YES		YES	YES		YES		
N. Ireland Western	YES	YES		YES				
Neath and Port Talbot	YES	YES	YES	YES				
Newcastle upon Tyne	YES	YES	YES	YES			YES	ILL
Newham	YES	YES	YES					
Newport								
Norfolk	YES	YES	YES	YES	YES			
N.E. Lincolnshire	YES	YES		YES	YES			
North Lincolnshire	YES	YES		YES				
North Tyneside	YES	YES	YES	YES				
North Yorkshire	YES		YES	YES				
Northamptonshire	YES	YES						
Northumberland	YES		YES	YES	YES			
Nottinghamshire	YES	YES	YES	YES	YES		YES	
Oldham			YES	YES	YES	YES		
Oxfordshire	YES	YES	YES	YES	YES			
Perth and Kinross	YES	YES	YES	YES	YES		YES	
Portsmouth	YES	YES	YES		YES			
Powys								
Redcar and Cleveland	YES		YES	YES	YES			
Renfrewshire								
Rhondda	YES							
Richmond	YES	YES	YES	YES				
Rotherham	YES	YES	YES	YES	YES			Publishing
Sandwell	YES	YES		YES	YES			
Scottish Borders			YES	YES				
Sheffield	YES	YES	YES	YES	YES			
Shetland Islands	YES		YES		YES			
Shropshire	YES	YES	YES	YES	YES			

	Reference work	Professional development	E-mail	Exploration	Online database	System support	Cataloguing/ acquisitions	Other
Solihull	YES	YES	YES	YES		YES		Training
Somerset	YES		YES	YES		YES		
South Ayrshire	YES	YES	YES	YES	YES			
South Lanarkshire								
South Tyneside	YES	YES	YES	YES	YES			
Southampton	YES	YES	YES	YES	YES			
Southwark	YES	YES	YES	YES		YES		
Staffordshire	YES	YES	YES	YES				
Stirling				YES				
Stockport	YES							
Suffolk	YES	YES	YES	YES	YES	YES		
Sunderland	YES			YES				
Surrey	YES	YES	YES	YES	YES			
Sutton	YES	YES	YES	YES				
Swansea	YES	YES		YES				
Tameside	YES	YES	YES	YES	YES		YES	
Torfaen	YES	YES	YES	YES			YES	
Tower Hamlets	YES		YES	YES				
Trafford	YES	YES	YES	YES				
Wakefield	YES	YES	YES	YES				
Walsall	YES	YES	YES	YES	YES	YES	YES	Viscount
Waltham Forest	YES	YES	YES	YES				
Wandsworth	YES	YES		YES				
Warwickshire	YES	YES	YES	YES				
West Lothian	YES	YES	YES	YES				
West Sussex	YES	YES	YES		YES			
Westminster	YES	YES	YES	YES	YES	YES		
Wigan	YES	YES	YES	YES		YES		
Wiltshire						YES		
Wirral	YES	YES	YES	YES				
Wolverhampton	YES			YES	YES			
Wrexham	YES		YES	YES				
York Libraries	YES							

Appendix 2.6
Online databases

Authority	Online databases
Aberdeen	Inpadoc, World Patent Index
Bradford	Companies House, Dunn and Bradstreet, FT Profile
Bristol	Cross, ICC, INSPEC, Medline, Predicast Prompt
Bromley	Business and Industry, FT Profile, Reuters, Tenders Electronic Daily
Calderdale	Prestel
Cambridgeshire	Acompline, BNB (BLAISE), Euromonitor, FT Profile, ICC, Kompass Online, Library of Congress, Urbaline
Camden	FT Profile
Cheshire	Bioscience, Derwent World Patents Index, ICC, Medline, Pollute, Reuters, Standard and Poor, Waterloo Signature
Conwy	BLAISE
Cornwall	CCN, ICC, Profile
Croydon	CNN, Companies House, Profile, Reuters
Cumbria	BLAISE
Derbyshire	Dialog, FT Profile
Devon	Dialog, Kompass Online, Waterloo Signature
Dundee	Dunn and Bradstreet, D&B Market Identifying, Derwent World Patents Index, Medline, Trademaniac
Edinburgh	Datastar, Dialog, FT Profile
Enfield	CCN, Companies House
Essex	ECHO (TED), FT Profile
Flintshire	Kompass, FT Profile
Gateshead	BLAISE, ESA, FT Profile
Glasgow	ABI Inform, Business and Industry, Companies House Directory, PTS Prompt, Reuters
Gloucestershire	TELL ME
Hackney	Key British Enterprises, Market Research
Hammersmith and Fulham	British Library OPAC, BT Phonebase, ICC, Kompass, Lawtel
Hampshire	APILIT, CHEM ABS, Compendex, Conference Papers Index, INSPEC, Medline, Reuters, SIGLE
Hertfordshire	Textline
Kent	Dial Tech, LGCNET, PAMIS, UK Trade marks
Kingston upon Hull	Casesearch, CH Direct, Equifax, ICC, Medline
Kirklees	Kompass Online, Reuters
Leeds	Companies House Direct, Dun and Bradstreet, Medline, Textline, Trademark Scan
Leicester	FT Profile
Leicestershire	Accompline, FT Profile
Lincolnshire	BLAISE, Companies House Direct
Liverpool	Charuas (Companies House), Dun and Bradstreet, World Patent Index
Luton	ICC, Kompass UK
Middlesbrough	Corporate Profound, Datastar, HMSO, Profile
Milton Keynes	CCN 2000, Dialog, FT Profile
N. Ireland Belfast	ERIC, FT Profile, Trademark Scan, World Patent Index
Newcastle upon Tyne	General Company Information Knight Ridder
Newham	FT Profile
Norfolk	Dialog
Norfolk	FT Profile – newspapers
North Tyneside	BLAISE, Dialog
North Yorkshire	BLAISE
Northumberland	BLAISE, Infocheck
Nottinghamshire	CRO, Derwent WPI Patents, DTB select, Infocheck, Kompass UK/Europe, LISA, Medline/Embase
Oxfordshire	Infocheck

Portsmouth	Compendex, INSPEC, Other Tradenames, Patents WPI, UK Tradenames
Renfrewshire	TELL ME
Authority	Online databases
Rochdale	BLAISE, Datastar, Dialog
Sandwell	Infocheck, Kompass Online
Somerset	Corporate Profound, TELL ME
South Tyneside	Datastar, Waterlow
Southampton	Compendex, Dun and Bradstreet, ICC, Inspec, Kompass, LISA, UK News
Suffolk	BLAISE, Dialog, Infocheck
Surrey	First Search
Tameside	BLAISE, Embase, Infocheck, Medline, FT Profile, Waterlow
Tower Hamlets	BBIP, ICC, LOCIS
Trafford	Kompass, TELL ME
West Sussex	BMB, Medline, UK News
Westminster	UK News
Wiltshire	Datastar, Dialog
Wirral	Kompass Business Online
Wrexham	Compass, Dialog, Infocheck
York Libraries	Companies House Direct, Dun and Bradstreet, Infocheck, Jordans on Mercury

Appendix 2.7 Community information management

	Library management system	Teletext	PC/ DBMS	Word-proc.	Internet	Online staff	Online public	Printed copies
Aberdeen			YES			YES	YES	
Angus	YES					YES	YES	
Barnet	YES					YES	YES	
Barnsley		YES	YES	YES		YES		YES
Bath and N.E. Somerset				YES	YES		YES	YES
Bedfordshire			YES					YES
Berkshire			YES		YES	YES	YES	YES
Bexley		YES				YES		
Birmingham					YES	YES	YES	
Blaenau Gwent	YES					YES	YES	YES
Bolton			YES		YES	YES	YES	YES
Bournemouth		YES				YES	YES	
Bradford	YES		YES			YES	YES	YES
Brent	YES					YES	YES	
Bridgend	YES					YES	YES	
Brighton and Hove	YES		YES	YES	YES	YES	YES	YES
Bristol			YES			YES	YES	YES
Bromley					YES	YES		YES
Buckinghamshire	YES						YES	
Bury			YES	YES		YES		YES
Calderdale				YES		YES	YES	YES
Cambridgeshire					YES	YES	YES	
Camden	YES				YES	YES	YES	YES
Carmarthenshire	YES						YES	YES
Ceredigion			YES	YES				YES
Cheshire						YES		YES
Conwy	YES		YES		YES	YES	YES	YES
Cornwall	YES		YES			YES	YES	
Coventry			YES			YES		
Croydon			YES		YES	YES	YES	YES
Darlington	YES					YES	YES	
Derby	YES							
Derbyshire	YES					YES		YES
Devon			YES		YES	YES	YES	YES
Doncaster		YES				YES	YES	YES
Dorset		YES					YES	
Dudley	YES					YES	YES	YES
Dumfries and Galloway			YES			YES	YES	
Dundee	YES		YES			YES	YES	YES
Durham	YES					YES	YES	YES
Ealing		YES				YES	YES	
East Ayrshire					YES	YES	YES	
East Dunbartonshire			YES			YES	YES	
East Lothian			YES					YES
East Renfrew	YES					YES	YES	YES
East Riding of Yorkshire			YES			YES	YES	YES
East Sussex		YES				YES	YES	YES
Edinburgh			YES	YES	YES	YES		
Enfield	YES					YES	YES	
Essex			YES			YES	YES	

	Library management system	Teletext	PC/ DBMS	Wordproc.	Internet	Online staff	Online public	Printed copies
Falkirk	YES						YES	
Fife			YES			YES	YES	YES
Flintshire						YES		
Gateshead		YES	YES		YES	YES		YES
Glasgow			YES					
Gloucestershire		YES			YES	YES	YES	YES
Greenwich	YES					YES	YES	
Gwynedd	YES					YES	YES	
Hackney						YES	YES	
Hammersmith and Fulham			YES	YES	YES	YES	YES	YES
Hampshire					YES	YES	YES	YES
Haringey	YES					YES	YES	YES
Harrow	YES					YES		
Hartlepool	YES					YES		YES
Hereford and Worcester	YES					YES	YES	YES
Hertfordshire	YES					YES	YES	
Hillingdon	YES					YES	YES	
Hounslow		YES				YES	YES	YES
Inverclyde			YES			YES	YES	YES
Isle of Wight	YES			YES		YES	YES	YES
Islington			YES		YES	YES	YES	YES
Kensington and Chelsea	YES					YES	YES	YES
Kent		YES				YES	YES	
Kingston upon Thames	YES					YES	YES	
Kirklees			YES		YES			
Knowsley	YES					YES	YES	
Lambeth	YES					YES	YES	YES
Lancashire	YES	YES				YES	YES	YES
Leeds	YES				YES	YES	YES	
Leicester	YES					YES	YES	YES
Leicestershire		YES	YES			YES	YES	YES
Lewisham	YES					YES	YES	
Lincolnshire			YES					
Luton	YES					YES		YES
Manchester			YES			YES		YES
Merthyr Tydfil				YES				YES
Merton		YES				YES	YES	
Middlesbrough						YES		YES
Midlothian			YES			YES		YES
Milton Keynes						YES	YES	YES
Monmouthshire	YES					YES	YES	YES
Moray			YES					
Newcastle upon Tyne	YES					YES	YES	YES
Newham					YES		YES	
Norfolk			YES		YES	YES	YES	YES
North Somerset			YES			YES		YES
North Tyneside				YES				YES
North Yorkshire			YES			YES		YES
Northamptonshire		YES				YES	YES	
Nottinghamshire			YES			YES		
Oxfordshire					YES			
Poole		YES					YES	
Portsmouth			YES	YES		YES		
Redcar and Cleveland	YES					YES	YES	YES
Rhondda	YES					YES	YES	
Richmond		YES				YES	YES	
Rochdale	YES					YES	YES	
Rotherham		YES	YES	YES	YES	YES	YES	YES
Rutland	YES		YES					
Salford			YES	YES		YES		YES
Sandwell			YES			YES		YES

	Library management system	Teletext	PC/ DBMS	Wordproc.	Internet	Online staff	Online public	Printed copies
Scottish Borders								YES
Sefton	YES					YES	YES	YES
Sheffield	YES		YES	YES		YES	YES	YES
Shetland Islands			YES	YES	YES	YES	YES	YES
Shropshire		YES	YES			YES	YES	YES
Solihull		YES		YES				YES
Somerset	YES					YES	YES	YES
South Lanarkshire	YES		YES			YES	YES	YES
Southampton						YES		YES
Southwark			YES					
Staffordshire		YES	YES					
Stirling	YES					YES	YES	YES
Stockport						YES	YES	
Stockton	YES					YES		YES
Stoke on Trent			YES			YES	YES	YES
Suffolk	YES					YES	YES	YES
Sunderland	YES							
Surrey	YES					YES	YES	YES
Sutton	YES	YES				YES	YES	
Swindon	YES					YES		YES
Tameside			YES					YES
Torfaen	YES					YES	YES	
Trafford			YES			YES	YES	YES
Vale of Glamorgan	YES						YES	YES
Wakefield	YES					YES	YES	
Walsall			YES			YES		YES
Waltham Forest	YES	YES				YES	YES	
Wandsworth				YES				YES
Warwickshire			YES					YES
West Lothian	YES					YES	YES	
West Sussex	YES				YES	YES	YES	YES
Westminster	YES					YES	YES	YES
Wigan			YES		YES	YES		
Wiltshire	YES		YES			YES	YES	YES
Wirral	YES					YES	YES	YES
Wolverhampton			YES			YES		
York Libraries			YES			YES	YES	YES

Appendix 2.8
Electronic public information

	Software used	Access points	Web address
Barnsley	V Base	7	
Berkshire	Web Vision	90	http://dspace.dial.pipex.com/infonet/index.htm.
Birmingham		23	birmingham.gov.uk
Brighton and Hove		2	http://esussex.abasoff.co.uk
Bristol	Web based		Bristol Digital City
Buckinghamshire	ALS	16	
Calderdale	Incon/Access	6	
Cambridgeshire	Natural	32	http://www.camcnty.gov.uk
Camden	In development		CAMDEN PILOT Website www.camden.gov.uk
Croydon		15	www.croydon.gov.uk
Dorset	Editel	20	
Dumfries and Galloway	Taps	2	
Dundee	DS Galaxy	20	
Durham	Oracle	4	
East Dumbartonshire	SCIP	5	
East Sussex	Abacus	6	
Edinburgh	Access	54	Planned for Autumn 1997
Enfield			www.enfield.gov.uk
Falkirk	DS Galaxy	18	
Gateshead			http://wamses@unn.ac..uk
Gloucestershire	Abacus	80	http://www.gloscc.gov.uk
Hampshire	Hants net	90	http://www.hants.gov.uk
Hereford and Worcester	Netscape	8	
Hertfordshire			http://hertslib.hertocc.gov.uk
Islington	Netscape	5	ww.islington.gov.co
Kingston upon Hull	Abacus	26	
Lincolnshire	Web Vision	52	htp://www.lincolnshire.gov.uk
Liverpool	Netshift	1	liverpool.gov.uk
Manchester	Tardis	5	www.manchester.gov.uk
Newcastle upon Tyne			http://newcastle-city-council.gov.uk
Newham			www.newham.gov.uk
Norfolk	Web Vision	17	http://www.icon.norfolk.gov.uk
Nottinghamshire	Town Crier	12	http//ww.nottscc.gov.uk/cc/index.htm
Oxfordshire	Abacus		
Redcar and Cleveland	Citycard	7	
Richmond	Saturn	16	
Rotherham	Abacus	19	http://www.rotherham.gov.uk
Sandwell	In-house	1	
Shropshire	Lotus Notes		
Southampton	Taps	4	http://hants.gov.uk
Southwark	Netscape		
Staffordshire	Web Vision	23	
Vale of Glamorgan	Career info	2	
Warwickshire			http://www.warwickshire.gov.uk
West Sussex	Abacus	10	www.west sussex.gov.uk
Westminster		4	http://lirn.viscount.org.uk/earl/members/westminst
		702	

Appendix 3.1
Public access PCs

	Libraries with open learning PCs	Total PCs for open learning	Libraries with PCs for hire	Total PCs for hire	Training schemes available?
Aberdeenshire	6	8			
Angus	1	2			
Barnet	3	5	6	6	YES
Barnsley	15	50	15	50	YES
Berkshire	1	1	2	2	
Bexley	1	2			
Birmingham	6	14	1	12	YES
Blaenau Gwent	1	8			
Bolton	1	1	1	1	
Bradford	1	1	1	25	
Brent	2	16	4	18	
Brighton and Hove	1	2	1	3	
Bristol	1	1			
Bromley	2	3	2	4	
Bury	1	2	2	2	
Caerphilly	1	1			
Calderdale	1	2	1	2	
Cambridgeshire	2	8	1	4	YES
Camden	2	7	12	13	
Cardiff	2	2			
Carmarthenshire	3	3			YES
Ceredigion	1	1			
Cheshire	6	6	10	18	
Cornwall	1	1			YES
Coventry	2	5			
Croydon	3	8	3	10	YES
Cumbria	8	15	10	15	
Denbighshire	3	3			YES
Derbyshire	1	1			
Devon	2	2			
Doncaster	1	1			
Dudley	1	3			YES
Dumfries and Galloway	1	1	1	1	
Dundee	1	2			YES
Durham	5	9			YES
East Ayrshire	2	2	4	4	
East Dumbartonshire	1	1			YES
East Lothian			2	2	YES
East Sussex	3	8	2	2	YES
Edinburgh	3	3	15	25	
Enfield	2	6	2	4	
Essex	3	6			
Fife	2	8			YES
Flintshire	2	4			
Gateshead	1	1			
Glasgow	18	19	22	23	
Gloucestershire	5	5			
Greenwich	1	2			
Hackney	7	4	7	14	
Hammersmith and Fulham	1	2			

	Libraries with open learning PCs	Total PCs for open learning	Libraries with PCs for hire	Total PCs for hire	Training schemes available?
Haringey	2	6	1	12	YES
Havering	1	3	3	3	
Hereford and Worcester	2	2			
Hertfordshire					YES
Highland	9	10			
Hillingdon	1	1			
Hounslow	1	1	1	6	YES
Inverclyde	1	1			
Isle of Wight	1	2			YES
Islington	3	6			YES
Kensington and Chelsea	2	4	2	2	YES
Kent	3	7			
Kingston upon Thames	1	7			YES
Kirklees	2	2			
Knowsley	7	14			
Lancashire	3	12			
Leeds	2	4			
Leicestershire	1	1			
Lewisham	2	16			
Lincolnshire	5	14		2	
Liverpool	2	2			
Luton	1	2			
Manchester	7	25			
Merthyr Tydfil	1	5			
Merton	1	3	1		YES
Midlothian	1	1			
Monmouthshire	1	1	1	1	YES
Moray	5	14			YES
N. Ireland North Eastern	1	3			YES
N. Ireland South Eastern	4				YES
Neath and Port Talbot	1	1			
Newcastle upon Tyne	1	3	5	7	
Newham	2	2	2	2	
Newport	5	8			
Norfolk	2	2			
North Ayrshire	2	4			
North East Lincolnshire			1	6	
North Lincolnshire	1	2	3	5	
North Tyneside	1	1	3	3	
Northamptonshire	2	2			
Northumberland	1	1	1	1	
Nottinghamshire	4	7	1	1	
Oldham	1	2			
Pembrokeshire	1	1	1	1	
Perth and Kinross	1	2	1	2	YES
Powys	5	6	5	6	YES
Redbridge	1	5			
Redcar and Cleveland	1	1			
Renfrewshire	1	1	15	17	
Rhondda	2	2			
Rochdale	1	2			
Rotherham	5	20			YES
Salford	1	3	1	1	YES
Sandwell	1	1			
Sefton	13	13			
Sheffield	5	10			
Shetland Islands	2	4			YES
Shropshire	4	6	25	30	YES
Solihull	1	7	1	7	YES
Somerset	1	1	0	0	
South Ayrshire			7	32	YES

	Libraries with open learning PCs	Total PCs for open learning	Libraries with PCs for hire	Total PCs for hire	Training schemes available?
South Gloucestershire	2	4			YES
South Lanarkshire	4	8			YES
South Tyneside	1	1			
Southampton	1	2	1	2	
Southwark			2	2	
St Helens	2	2			
Staffordshire	6	17			YES
Stirling	1	1			
Stockport	13	16			
Stoke on Trent	1	3			
Suffolk	1	2			
Sunderland	2	24			
Surrey	6	30	7	28	YES
Sutton	2	2	1	8	YES
Swansea	2	2			
Tameside	2	6			
Torfaen	2	2	3	3	
Trafford	2	2			
Vale of Glamorgan	1	1	5	6	
Wakefield	2	4			
Walsall	1	2			
Waltham Forest	1	4			
Wandsworth			7	7	
Warwickshire	2	3			YES
West Dumbarton	1	4			
West Lothian	1	1			
Westminster	1	2	1	1	
Wigan	4	6			
Wiltshire	1	1			
Wirral	5	10	5	10	
Wrexham	1	1			
	354	720	240	474	

Appendix 3.2 Telecentres

Authority	Description
Berkshire	Input/Output – general service at Reading Library
Birmingham	Input/Output in Central library
Bradford	See leaflet
Bristol	Input/Output – currently negotiating
Cambridgeshire	Input/Output – Cambridge Library; open learning centre – Peterborough
Camden	Tendering process for computer centre at the Central Library
Conwy	Discussion with local FE college to set up Cyberskills centre with ICL
Coventry	Input/Output planned for Central Library
Croydon	Currently under consideration
Cumbria	Video conferencing in two libraries for public/business use
Denbighshire	Learning Resource Centre at Rhyl Library during 1997–8
Doncaster	Planning Ramesis/Input/Output type centre
Dumfries and Galloway	IT Centre in one library planned for 1997 – European part-funded
Ealing	Input/Output centre planned for Autumn 1997 at Central Library
East Ayrshire	Proposal for the establishment of computing facilities in all libraries
East Lothian	Plan for open learning centre – charities lottery bid with FE college
East Riding of Yorkshire	IT centre planned for Goole Library in Autumn with Community Education
Glasgow	Video conferencing; Telecities project; Glasgow telecollege network
Gwynedd	Library in building with community development agency telecentre
Hammersmith and Fulham	Input/Output centre provision is being explored
Haringey	Computer centre in Central Library with Haringey Educ training agency
Hillingdon	Planned for Central Library Autumn 1997 with training and Internet access
Hounslow	Input/Output Centre – Hounslow Library. Funding for 6 others sought
Islington	Input/Output Centre due to open in Central Library August 1997
Kensington and Chelsea	Input/Output Centre
Kent	Planned for 1997–8
Kingston upon Thames	Plans for telecentre in Tolworth library in co-operation with Aztec
Kirklees	Negotiating with private company for IT centre at Huddersfield
Leeds	Input/Output due Central Library in June 1997
Lincolnshire	Telecentre Alford Library run by private company
Liverpool	Hope to open telecentre-type facility this year
Luton	Input/Output Centre or similar inhouse with Community Services
Manchester	IT centres in 6 libraries
Merton	Input/Output Centre at Wimbledon
Milton Keynes	Input/Output Centre planned
Monmouthshire	'Monmouthshire ONLINE' project will provide centres in 4 libraries
Newcastle upon Tyne	Plans to develop this facility within the next calendar year.
North Tyneside	Working with our catering section to set up cybercafé in Central Library
Northumberland	Under investigation
Oxfordshire	Input/Output Centre
Portsmouth	Initial planning stage
Powys	One existing Telecentre due to move into a branch library
Redbridge	Input/Output being explored
Richmond	Input/Output Centre at Richmond Library
Rutland	Telecentre at Oakham Library planned subject to partnership funding
Solihull	IT POINT – public access IT facility at Chelmsley wood library
Somerset	Libnet centres at Taunton (with GEAC) and Street libraries
South Ayrshire	South Ayrshire Cybercentres in 3 libraries
Southampton	Business planning currently under way
Sunderland	Plan to establish a cybercafé on a partnership basis
Surrey	Possibly unite adult education IT facilities with library learning centres
Sutton	Input/Output Centre – Central Library

Authority	Description
Swansea	Currently investigating feasibility
Tameside	CAPS – council access points in two libraries as a pilot scheme
Walsall	Telstart learning centre planned for Bloxwich library with Walsall College
Waltham Forest	Partnership with Systems Express Ltd at Leytonstone library
Wandsworth	Input/Output Centre scheduled to start in Autumn 1997
West Sussex	Plans for an Input/Output centre in 1 library
Westminster	Input/Output at 2 libraries

Appendix 4.1
Charges for Internet access

Authority	Charges
Aberdeen	£2.50 per half hour
Barnsley	Free
Bath and North East Somerset	Approximately £5 per hour
Bedfordshire	£2 per half hour, £3 per hour
Berkshire	£2.50 per half hour
Birmingham	Charges as levied by Input/Output
Bradford	No charge for enquiry; public access as per Ramesis charges
Brent	Free to all library members but sessions must be booked
Bridgend	£1.75 – half hour £2.75 – 1 hour, printing 10p per A4
Brighton and Hove	£1.50 for half hour incl. 5 free pages printout
Caerphilly	1st hour free. Thereafter £1.25 per 30 mins. £2.00 per hour
Calderdale	£2 per 20 minutes; £1 per 10 minutes thereafter
Cambridgeshire	Access free, considering charges for e-mail and downloading
Cardiff	£2.50 half hour, printouts 10p, £4.50 hour
Cheshire	£2.50 for 30 mins, £1.25 concessions
Conwy	£2.50 per half hour, free if staff use to answer enquiry
Cornwall	Will probably charge £5 per hour
Croydon	£5 per hour; £2.50 concessions
Cumbria	£5 per hour introductory training session (c.45 mins) £2.50
Denbighshire	Charging to be introduced. £2.50 per half hour to cover line costs
Devon	Free
Dumfries and Galloway	£5.00 per 55 minute session, £3.00 per 25 minute session
Dundee	£2.50 per half hour, £1.90 per half hour concession
East Ayrshire	£3 per hour, £2 per half hour
East Sussex	£1.50 per half hour session.
Edinburgh	Free; (downloading also free); printout: 20p per page
Enfield	Per 25 minute session: tutored £3, £2.50 conc. Untutored £2, £1.50 conc.
Essex	Free
Flintshire	Free
Gloucestershire	Free
Hampshire	£5 per hour viewing; printouts at 30p each
Hertfordshire	£3 half hour, £5 per hour
Hounslow	Charged through Input/Output
Isle of Wight	£3 per half hour, £5 per hour
Islington	Free
Kingston upon Hull	Free
Kingston upon Thames	£1.50 per hour on WWW. 10p per sheet printing. 75p floppy to download
Leicestershire	£1 per half hour
Lewisham	Free access
Lincolnshire	£3 per hour
Luton	£2.50 per half hour; £2.25 advantage card; £1.50 a card + students
Manchester	£2 per hour after 6pm, £ 2.50 per hour before 6pm
Midlothian	Free
Monmouthshire	£1.50 per 30 minutes; £2.50 per hour, printout 10p, disks £1.50
Moray	£2 per half hour, £3.50 per hour
N. Ireland North Eastern	Free
N. Ireland South Eastern	Printouts only 20p per sheet
Neath and Port Talbot	£4.50 per hour
Newcastle upon Tyne	£5.00 per hour for non-residents
Newport	£3 per half hour, £1.50 for holders of Council leisure pass
Norfolk	£2 per 30 mins, 20p per sheet printout
North East Lincolnshire	£1 per hour

Authority	Charges
North Lincolnshire	£5.20 per hour, £2.20 concessions
Perth and Kinross	£2.50 per 30 minutes
Powys	hourly rate
Redcar and Cleveland	Free
Rhondda	£2 per hour
Richmond	Charges levied by Input/Output
Rotherham	To start in July WWW access only approx £3 per hour, less for concessions
Sandwell	50p per half hour session
Shropshire	£4 per hour, £2 per hour concessions.
Solihull	£5 per hour
Somerset	£3 per half hour, £2 concessions, 10p printout, £10 pa e-mail box
South Ayrshire	£3 per hour
South Lanarkshire	£1 for 15 minutes
Southampton	£5.00 per hour; pilot stage
Southwark	£3 per hour, printing 5p per page
Stockport	£3 per hour peak time, £2.50 off peak, £1.50 leisure card holders, print 12p.
Suffolk	5p printout
Sunderland	£5 per hour, £2.50 per half hour
Surrey	Free, 10p printout
Sutton	Via Input/Output – £5 per hour
Swansea	£2.50 per half hour
Torfaen	£1.50 per half hour for Web access; 50p to send/receive e-mail
Warwickshire	£1 per half hour; 30p for prints
Westminster	Free
Wirral	£2.50 per half hour
York Libraries	Free half hour sessions only

Appendix 4.2
Charges for public access PCs

Authority	Charges
Barnet	£3.50 per hour
Barnsley	Free
Berkshire	£1.50 per hour
Bexley	Free
Birmingham	Free access to open learning
Bolton	Charged per bookable session
Bradford	Ramesis charges
Brent	Sessions must be booked and charges vary from different libraries
Bridgend	£1.25 per hour for word-processing
Brighton and Hove	£1.50 per half hour
Bury	£1 per hour + £1 per disc
Calderdale	Free
Cambridgeshire	Various
Camden	Up to £5 hour; average cost £2.50 per hour
Cheshire	£1 per hour, 50p concessions
Croydon	£5 per hour, £2.50 concessions
Cumbria	£1 per hour for word-processing use etc., free for reference to CD-ROM
Devon	£2.50 per hour for word-processing
Doncaster	Free
Dumfries and Galloway	£2.00 per 55 minute session
Dundee	Free
East Ayrshire	Free. Service bookable for 1 hour or half hour slots
East Lothian	Free
Edinburgh	Free access
Enfield	Wordprocessing £2 per hour; disks £1.50; printouts 10p, £1 colour
Essex	Free
Flintshire	Free
Glasgow	£2 per hour; includes disk and paper supply for printer
Gloucestershire	Free, 10p per sheet printout
Greenwich	Free
Haringey	£3 per hour, £12 membership
Havering	£4 per hour hire charge
Hounslow	Charged through Input/Output
Isle of Wight	Free
Kent	Free
Kirklees	Free, prints 20p per sheet
Leicestershire	Free
Lewisham	Free
Liverpool	Free
Manchester	Free
Merthyr Tydfil	Free
Merton	Charges set by Input/Output centre
Midlothian	Free
Monmouthshire	£1.50 per half hour, £2.50 per hour, 10p per print out, disks £1.50
N. Ireland North Eastern	Free
N. Ireland Southern	£2.00 per hour
Newcastle upon Tyne	£1.50 per hour, 70p per 30 minutes word-processing
Newham	Free, charge for printing page 20p
Newport	Free
North East Lincolnshire	£1 per hour plus printing
North Lincolnshire	Free, print 30p per sheet
North Tyneside	£ 2.50 per hour

Authority	Charges
Nottinghamshire	Word-processing: £1.50 per 90 minute session
Oldham	Free
Pembrokeshire	50p per floppy disk, £3.00 per hour for hire, 10p per A4 sheet printout
Perth and Kinross	50p for 30 minutes
Powys	Hourly rate
Redcar and Cleveland	Free
Rhondda	Free
Richmond	Input/Output centre
Rochdale	Free
Rotherham	Free, charge for printing
Salford	Free, 10p for printout, £1 per disk
Sandwell	50p for half hour session when service commences
Sefton	Free, charge for printing only
Sheffield	Free, only print cost
Shropshire	£2 per hour
Solihull	£2.50 per hour
Somerset	£2.50 per half hour, £2 concession
South Ayrshire	£2 per hour
Southampton	Free; part of Open Learning facility; 10p per page print; diskette charge
Southwark	£2 per hour, printout 5p per page
St Helens	Free
Stockport	Free, 12p printing.
Sunderland	Free
Surrey	£1– £3.50 per hour
Sutton	Input/Output
Swansea	Free
Torfaen	50p per half hour, 10p per printout
Vale of Glamorgan	Free, printing – 10p b/w, 20p colour
Wandsworth	£3.50 per hour
West Dumbarton	Free
West Lothian	Free
Westminster	£4 first hour, £2 subsequent hours
Wigan	Free
Wirral	Free, £1 per floppy disk for use on PC

Appendix 4.3 Charges for CD-ROM

Authority	Charges
Aberdeen	Free
Angus	Free
Barnet	Free, but printing at 20p per page
Barnsley	Free
Bedfordshire	Free access, printing 20p black and white, 30p colour
Berkshire	Free
Bexley	Free for reference, loans from central library £2 per 7 days
Birmingham	£1 for 3 nights, £2 for 7 nights, free for reference
Blaenau Gwent	Free for reference, charge for printing, CD-ROM charged weekly
Bolton	Access free, charge for printing
Bournemouth	Staff use only, 10p per sheet for printout
Bradford	Free
Brent	Charges apply to printing and vary between locations
Bridgend	Free – no downloading to floppy, printing allowed at 10p per A4
Brighton and Hove	Free for use, 50p per A4 printout
Bristol	Free access, printing 20p per sheet
Bromley	Ft Extel £1.03, Keynote market research £3.00
Buckinghamshire	Free to use, charge for printing
Bury	Free
Caerphilly	Loan £2.00 per week
Calderdale	Free for reference, loan 80p to £1.60 per week
Cambridgeshire	Free for reference, printing 30p per sheet
Camden	Free access, charge for print
Cardiff	Printouts 10p each A4
Carmarthenshire	50p
Ceredigion	Printouts 10p per sheet
Cheshire	Loan £2 per week (£1.50 conc)
City of London	Charge for printing 30p per page
Conwy	Free other than for printouts
Cornwall	Various – free to search, pay for printouts generally about £3.50
Coventry	£2 for loan, concessions available
Croydon	Free to search, page printout 20p
Cumbria	Free for reference use, lending charge £1.50 per week
Denbighshire	Free, booking procedure, requiring proof of identity
Devon	£2.00 per week, fines £1.50 per week to a maximum of £9.00
Doncaster	Free
Dumfries and Galloway	Loan charge £2.00 per week
Dundee	First 10 sheets of printout free, then 10p per page
East Ayrshire	CD-ROMs for reference use only, free
East Sussex	To lend £2, free for reference, printout 20p per page
Edinburgh	Free access, printout 20p per page
Enfield	Free for reference, printouts 10p
Essex	Loan £1.99 3 weeks, printouts 10p per page
Falkirk	Printing charge only
Fife	Print charge 10p per page
Flintshire	Free use in library
Glasgow	Free, b/w prints 10p, colour 40p
Gloucestershire	Free, printout 10p per sheet
Gwynedd	Free
Hackney	Charges at 5p per sheet for all services
Hampshire	Free viewing, prints at 10p
Harrow	10p printout

Authority	Charges
Hertfordshire	Free access
Isle of Wight	Free
Kensington and Chelsea	Loan £1.50 per week, free for reference, printing 20p per page
Kent	Free, 10p per sheet printing
Kingston upon Hull	Printing 10p per sheet
Kirklees	Prints 20p per sheet, lending £2 per week
Knowsley	Printing only 10p per sheet b/w, 50p per colour sheet
Lambeth	Free to use
Leeds	Free
Leicester	20p per sheet for printouts
Leicestershire	Free
Lewisham	Free
Lincolnshire	£1.50 per week for loans
Liverpool	Printing 35p per sheet
Luton	£1.50 for 1 week's hire
Manchester	Loan £1.50 per week
Merthyr Tydfil	Free (ex-printing)
Merton	Charge per sheet printed 2p
Midlothian	Free
Milton Keynes	£1.50 or £2 for 2 weeks loan
Monmouthshire	Free, 10p print charges
N. Ireland North Eastern	Free
N. Ireland South Eastern	Printouts only 20p per sheet
N. Ireland Southern	Ramesis CD-ROM collection
Neath and Port Talbot	5p per printout
Newcastle upon Tyne	Printouts 20p per sheet
Newham	Free access inhouse
Newport	Free
Norfolk	20p printouts
North East Lincolnshire	Free, printout 25p
North Lincolnshire	30p printout b/w, 35p printout in colour
North Somerset	Charge for copies made 20p
North Tyneside	Free
Northamptonshire	Printout 35p per page, lending £2.05 per week
Nottinghamshire	Free
Oldham	CD-ROM loans £2 per week, reference use free, printing 10p per sheet
Oxfordshire	Search fee £5.00, prints 50p, disk copies £10.00, annual sub £50.00
Pembrokeshire	Free to use, 10p per sheet printout
Perth and Kinross	Loans £2.00 p.w. per item
Poole	Use free, printing 10p persheet
Portsmouth	Charge for printing only, loan collection (lending) £1.50–2.00.
Redcar and Cleveland	Printouts 10p
Rhondda	Free for use in library
Richmond	10p per page
Rochdale	Free
Rotherham	Free to use, charges to borrow, charge for printing
Salford	10p for printout
Sandwell	Free
Scottish Borders	£1.50 per week hire charge
Solihull	Free
Somerset	10p printout
South Ayrshire	Free
South Gloucestershire	Printouts 10p b/w, 20p for colour
South Lanarkshire	Free
South Tyneside	Loan 70p per 2 weeks
Southampton	Free for use, 10p per page printing
Southwark	Free for use, printout 5p per page
St Helens	Free
Staffordshire	Printouts 10p per sheet
Stockport	Free, 12p printing
Stoke on Trent	Lending £2 per week, free for reference, printouts 10p
Suffolk	5p printout
Sunderland	Free

Authority	Charges
Surrey	Hire £2 per week, free for reference, printout 10p
Swansea	Printing costs only
Swindon	Loan charge £1.50
Tameside	Free
Torfaen	Loan charge £2.50 per item
Vale of Glamorgan	10p b/w, 20p colour
Waltham Forest	25p per printout
Warwickshire	Free for use CD-ROM, 30p for prints
West Dumbarton	Free
Westminster	Free, printing at 10p
Wigan	Free
Wirral	Free
Wolverhampton	Printout charges only (20p)
Wrexham	10p per printout
York Libraries	Charge from KBE200 for mailing lists, otherwise 10p per A4 sheet

Appendix 4.4
Open learning charges

Authority	Charges
Angus	Free
Barnet	£15 per year, £10 concession
Barnsley	Free, except for overdue charges
Berkshire	£20 for a whole year's use
Bexley	Annual subscription of £20 or £10 for 1 course
Birmingham	Free
Blaenau Gwent	Free
Bradford	Free
Brent	Annual fee of £20 waged, £10 unwaged
Brighton and Hove	£10 for 6 months (£5 concessions)
Bromley	Loan fees £3 per week
Bury	Free
Caerphilly	Free
Calderdale	40p per 3 weeks (passport to leisure 20p)
Cambridgeshire	Various
Camden	£25.00 p.a. (£12.50 p.a. concessions)
Cardiff	Free
Cheshire	Free
Coventry	Free, printout at 10p per sheet
Croydon	£20 per annum, £10 concessions
Denbighshire	Free, booking procedure requiring proof of identity.
Derbyshire	Free
Devon	Free
Doncaster	Free
Dumfries and Galloway	Free
Dundee	Free
East Dumbartonshire	Free
East Sussex	Free
Edinburgh	Free, printing: 5 sheets free, then 1p per sheet
Enfield	Annual subscription £20, concessions £10, printouts 10p per sheet.
Essex	Free
Flintshire	Free
Glasgow	Free
Gloucestershire	Free
Greenwich	Free
Hammersmith and Fulham	Subscription yearly
Hounslow	Free (part of council Anti-poverty strategy)
Isle of Wight	Free
Islington	Free
Kent	Free
Kingston upon Thames	Operated by Kingston community education
Kirklees	Free, prints 20p per sheet
Leeds	Free
Leicestershire	Free
Lewisham	Free
Manchester	Free
Merthyr Tydfil	Free
Merton	£20 per annum subscription
Midlothian	Free
Milton Keynes	£1 or £2 for 2 weeks loan
Monmouthshire	Free
N. Ireland North Eastern	Free

Authority	Charges
N. Ireland South Eastern	Free
Neath and Port Talbot	Free
Newcastle upon Tyne	Free
Newham	Free, charge for printing page 20p
Newport	Free
Norfolk	Annual registration fee £5 to borrow items
North Lincolnshire	Cassette loan 55p adults, 25p concessions, video £1.65
North Tyneside	Free
Northamptonshire	50p per hour for use of PC, £2.20 for loan of multimedia pack
Nottinghamshire	Free
Oldham	Free
Pembrokeshire	Free
Perth and Kinross	Free
Powys	Free
Redbridge	Free in library, £1.00 per loan for open learning pack
Redcar and Cleveland	Free in library, hire of packages £3 for 4 weeks
Rhondda	Free
Richmond	Free loan collection at 1 library
Rochdale	Free
Rotherham	Free
Salford	Free,10p per printout, £1 per disk
Sandwell	Free
Shetland Islands	Free
Solihull	Free
South Ayrshire	Free
South Gloucestershire	Free
South Lanarkshire	Free
South Tyneside	Free
Southwark	Free
Staffordshire	Free
Stirling	Free, printouts 10p per sheet
Stockton	Free 12p printing
Suffolk	Free
Sunderland	Free
Surrey	Free
Sutton	£1–£3.50 per hour
Swansea	£20 p.a., £5 concessions
Swindon	Free
Torfaen	Free
Tower Hamlets	Free
Wakefield	Free
Wandsworth	Free
West Dumbarton	Free, 30p for prints
West Lothian	Free
West Sussex	Free
Wigan	£10 p.a. plus 20% resident cardholder discount
Wiltshire	Free
Wolverhampton	Free

Appendix 4.5
Online search charges

Authority	Charges
Aberdeen	Cost recovery plus £15 if the search takes longer than 30 mins
Bedfordshire	Cost recovery + 10%
Berkshire	Only carried out by staff
Birmingham	Cost plus 10%
Bradford	Variable
Bridgend	Free
Brighton and Hove	£18 per half hour
Bristol	Cost –50% in ref library cost +10% in commercial library
Bromley	Cost of online search + 10% + staff time charge: £30.76
Buckinghamshire	Cost recovery basis if asked to do search
Calderdale	Printouts only 10p per page
Cambridgeshire	Actual cost (connect cost and printouts)
Camden	Free (at discretion of as to whether use is appropriate)
Carmarthenshire	£2 per hour
Cheshire	£15 plus connect/search costs
City of London	Fee based service only
Cornwall	£3.50 per search and downloading at cost
Coventry	Bibliographies: no charge; company information at cost
Croydon	£30 per hour, plus connection and format charges where appropriate
Cumbria	Free, production of mailing lists is charged for
Denbighshire	Facilitated via Flintshire library and information service reference dept
Derbyshire	Company searches £30, other searches cost plus £5 standing charge
Devon	Based on actual cost and staff time and admin (+VAT)
Dundee	Cost of search plus 10%
East Riding of Yorkshire	Cost + 10%
East Sussex	£15.50 per half hour min., £10; costs incurred.
Edinburgh	Detailed search and downloads charged at service provider rate
Enfield	Various charges generally at cost plus 25%, printouts 10p per sheet
Essex	At cost where charged limited use by staff on behalf of users
Flintshire	Cost recovery
Gateshead	Varied occasional transfer of costs only to customer
Glasgow	Cost + VAT + connect charge of £0.05 per minute (minimum £10)
Gloucestershire	£20 per hour + actual charges: in-depth searches; quick search free
Hammersmith and Fulham	Cost recovery
Hampshire	Free if staff decision, or else £1 per minute and £10 + 25p per print
Kent	Cost recovery: £12+ per search
Kingston upon Hull	Varies according to type of search and customer from £1 to £55 + VAT
Kirklees	Cost recovery
Leicester	4p per line, 40p per minute
Leicestershire	Cost + 20% for staff time + VAT
Lewisham	No charge
Lincolnshire	Dependent on size ; £1 per line approx.
Liverpool	£21 + 10% handling charge
Luton	Cost + 10% of VAT
Middlesbrough	Staff time plus online time
Midlothian	None
Milton Keynes	Variable
N. Ireland Belfast	Public: first £10 free; corporate: full cost recovery
N. Ireland North Eastern	Free
Newcastle upon Tyne	£30.00 per hour, minimum £15.00
Newham	Free
Norfolk	Access costs plus 25%

Authority	Charges
North East Lincolnshire	At cost plus 10%
North Tyneside	No charge
Northamptonshire	£1 connection charge + cost of search + handling charge of 35%
Nottinghamshire	Cost + 20% + VAT; mailing lists: 15p per record (lower for 1000 + records)
Oldham	Minimum £1 charged at cost
Oxfordshire	£5.50 + VAT, minimum £10.00
Portsmouth	On demand £10 + online/print costs, free with staff discretion
Rochdale	Searched by staff: no charge
Rotherham	Only available in Buarim library, charge for searching and printing
Sandwell	Full company report £25, snapshot report £15
Sheffield	Full cost recovery plus staff reasearch
Somerset	£20 flat rate
Southampton	At staff discretion, charges per cost of hits + £10 basic fee
Stoke on Trent	Full cost + VAT
Suffolk	Business users pay full cost of search, others pay 10p per printout
Surrey	Free
Tameside	Free
Trafford	Pass on Kompass and Tell Me charges plus cost of printouts
Warwickshire	£10 standard search, non-standard £10 + database print costs + VAT
West Sussex	First 5 minutes free then according to the database used
Westminster	Cost + markup
Wiltshire	By agreement with Information Manager
Wirral	10p per 5 minutes
Wrexham	Cost recovery basis
York Libraries	Cost of search + 10% + VAT

Appendix 5.1 Management and training arrangements

Authority	Management and training arrangements
Aberdeen	No formal training of specialist staff. They attend courses and seminars as appropriate. The systems and multimedia librarians provide IT training sessions for front line staff when requested.
Aberdeenshire	Automated library system and LIBRIS OPAC are the responsibility of the Stock/Computer Services Librarian assisted by the Bibliographic Services Librarian and two Assistant Librarians.
Angus	2 senior librarians share the responsibility for management of the system, and they coordinate staff training. Technical support is provided by supplier and the council's IT department.
Barnet	IT management by 2 technical staff with support from corporate computer department. IT training by corporate IT training staff, local colleges, Library Association courses and in-house training.
Barnsley	Technical management: public systems – some maintained by the local college, some by local authority. Acorn computers maintained by the local school. Computer services librarian deals with day to day management. Library system – partially managed by the local authority IT department. Library staff are the first line managers of the system. Training – IT, Internet/e-mail training by the local college and local authority. Library management system – in-house training
Bath and N.E. Somerset	System managed by Bristol.
Bedfordshire	Separate specialist team within the Department of Education Arts and Libraries provides support and training – no formal system.
Berkshire	Courses, cascade training.
Bexley	The Dynix computer is operated on behalf of the library service by Syntax, facilities management consultants. Within the libraries department there are 2 full time systems staff who report direct to the head of the library provider unit, and who are responsible for the day to day management of the Dynix system and other libraries' IT equipment. Training is received annually and arranged in-house. All aspects of system management are being reviewed this year with a view to developing a formal department IT strategy.
Birmingham	1 Library systems – specialist systems manager 2 EPIS/WWW – 2 X project managers Staff training handled in many different ways.
Blaenau Gwent	System controlled in liaison with county borough IT Department. Information officer acts as systems librarian for the library service.
Bolton	2 specialist staff to coordinate management and support of systems. System centre – FM-based.
Bournemouth	1 'PALS' managed as a joint arrangement by Bournemouth and Dorset. IT departments with reporting on faults channelled through Bournemouth Libraries' Systems Support Officer. 2. CD-ROM/Internet policy managed by information services librarian. 3. Word-processing and office systems managed by Bournemouth Borough IT department. 4. Regional library system CD-ROM/UNITY managed by principal librarian, support services, in consultation with SWRLS and LIBRIS. 5. IT training coordinated by Bournemouth Libraries' principal librarian, support services liaising with appropriate library and IT staff.
Bradford	Currently under review – management of systems. Free training of library staff via Ramesis system.
Brent	Library system is managed on FM contract. Staff training and awareness. Courses at basic and advanced level on the Internet. Search skills made available to key staff. Training is cascaded at branch level. (Ongoing skills audit to determine needs of staff and the scope of the service).

Authority	Management and training arrangements
Bridgend	The LAN is maintained by the computer company that installed it, though day to day problems are solved by information officer (library staff). Apart from information officer who was trained by GEAC – staff are trained in-house and given time to familiarize themselves with Internet, CD-ROMs etc. Library automation system is managed by library staff – no specialists.
Brighton and Hove	IT support (technical) is provided by central council IT support team. Networks in 2 central libraries managed by library staff but rely on central IT support. Training provided in-house by library staff and by IT support staff, and using external courses (where funds allow). New strategy being drawn up to take account of new library computer system (due Dec 1997).
Bristol City Council	Systems Team, Libraries IT group within Library Service currently in operation.
Bromley	1 Staff training has traditionally been done with a mix of in-house training and external courses 2 There are plans to allocate a full-time trainer as part of our IT roll out of projects.
Buckinghamshire	Specialist staff = 1 X technical services assistant. Library support operations manager is responsible for strategic overview. Working group responsible for ensuring IT training for branch staff.
Bury	Technical management – support from council information services department. No particular specialist staff on establishment, (1 senior manager on secondment for circulation/catalogue system). Staff training – ongoing on-site training as and when required.
Calderdale	No specialist staff. Library staff manage basic problems, calling on the council's IT department or SB Electronics for any problems more advanced. Staff training is done at a basic level to cope with everyday use of systems.
Cambridgeshire	Technical – In-house IT unit (3 FTEs). Service level agreements for support of: • DYNIX library automation system • Network maintenance and installation (from FM contractor) • PC Installation and maintenance (from corporate IT department) Training – In-house training in the use of the library automation system PC, Windows, Internet, word-processing training purchased from education IT agency.
Camden	Support through LMS contract with supplier and in-house expertise. Training and awareness through publication of bulletins reflecting changes.
Cardiff	We have a computer maintenance team of two; training is provided to staff in new developments before they are instituted; more detailed and extensive training is given to staff who will be using new systems.
Carmarthenshire	Training organized with suppliers.
Cheshire	Bought-in courses and interactive packages.
City of London	Posts of system manager and assistant system manager support all technical applications training provided by central IT department for Microsoft Office. Other training done in-house.
Conwy	1 County Borough Council's IT section in same directorate as LIS and close cooperation in particular with hardware acquisition and maintenance 2 talNet manages BLCMP Talis system on behalf of the supplier 3 Post of special services librarian has role of IT development 4 IT team (who produced strategy) meet 3 times a year (includes representative from IT section) to suggest developments and to monitor activities. 5 TNA is expected to address ad hoc nature of staff training and awareness.
Cornwall	Courses as required – either external or in-house.
Coventry	Systems Librarian and technical assistant provide full system support at present. All but TALIS software support will pass to Council's IT provider in near future. Staff training is carried out by senior staff in branch libraries.
Croydon	Library management system – staffed by one full time member of staff and 2 part time librarians plus clerical help. All front of house staff trained in-house on the job. In-house manuals produced. Weekly meeting with all service managers includes update and discussion of system matters as appropriate. PC systems – 2 full time staff.
Denbighshire	1 Technical Management is provided by the IT Department of Denbighshire County Council. 2 An ongoing training plan meets the needs of staff development in relation to library circulation system, CD-ROM facilities, and Internet.
Derby	Derbyshire county council IT team look after hardware-software under joint agreement.
Derbyshire	County Council computer Division responsible for hardware, software and some training. Departmental responsibilities are for routine hardware matters and some staff training. Hardware maintenance is contracted out, software support is in-house.

Authority	Management and training arrangements
Devon	Library based specialist team, providing help desk, support, acquisition of hardware and software, training and advice. Staff also liaise with corporate unit and main help-desk and direct with system suppliers. Production of in-house manuals and training. Devon IT services (a county council business unit) also offer training and awareness sessions.
Doncaster	GEAC 9000 housed in Council's computer section. Day to day operations carried out by computer section staff. Systems Librarian monitors the system software and hardware performance and monitors response to fault reports. Any special programs required are run by Systems Librarian, or by GEAC.
Dorset	1 County Council project team. 2 2 X Departmental senior managers with responsibility for systems: (a) Library Management (b) Reference and Information Services. 3 Continuous training as system develops for staff at all levels.
Dudley	Information services officer – for technical management. Staff training – undertaken by information services officer or via the council's IT department.
Dumfries and Galloway	No specialist staff. Support from Council's Information Services and staff training in-house.
Dundee	The community information team has a system development worker who is responsible for the technical management of the system. Workplace training is provided between 9 and 10 a.m. on a Wednesday. Additional training is provided as required.
Ealing	Support for the library housekeeping system and the Abacus Community Information database is provided primarily by the computer operations librarian, who is assisted by other members of the Bibliographic Services Team. She also provides training for all new staff and refresher training as necessary.
East Ayrshire	Systems management: Unicorn – No specialist staff, system is managed by the senior librarian with software support from Sirsi; BookshelF – Councils IT department manage the system. Software support from BookshelF. Staff Training: Unicorn – Training provided by Sirsi, then cascaded, plus on the job training; PC etc. training and awareness – council-organized courses, then cascaded.
East Dumbartonshire	Library system – 2 people plus specialized staff with knowledge in their own area. CI – Carried out by SCIP with 2 members of reference staff carrying updates etc. Ongoing training programmes for staff.
East Lothian	In-house training of staff by council's IT section. Courses with F/E college.
East Renfrew	With new system have been using the cascade system with key trainers. Allowing staff to familiarize themselves with the system – each member treated as an individual with different needs. As we move towards the Internet we are aware of the need for staff to be trained to the highest level.
East Riding	ALS system managed by PRISM joint arrangement. There are currently no specialist IT staff in post: 2 posts currently being established to manage community information and PC installations. IT reskilling programme in preparation.
East Sussex	IT support officer supports all the library IT systems, now part of a larger department known as Legal and Community services. The community information system is managed and supported by a single member of staff who works in conjunction with IT support officers.
Edinburgh	1 City of Edinburgh Council IT Dept. provides technical support 2 Library service has dedicated IT services development librarian. 3 Staff training courses for basic PC Awareness, Windows, MS-Office and INTERNET developed in partnership with local college 4 In-house arrangement for support include a contact list of 'computerate' persons, and a list of frequently asked questions.
Enfield	2 X specialist IT staff. Community information and council Website management by libraries first stop staff. Libraries system database management by various staff as part of their jobs. Internal user group – 1 open learning coordinator, 1 specialist Internet assistant. Management of IT resources and staff currently under corporate review. Staff training – mix of contractors supplied. Internal and external courses and DIY. Resource constraints preclude more desirable structured training.
Essex	All staff will be trained to use new library system. Technical staff will be trained.
Falkirk	Maintenance contract with DS Ltd. Systems librarian. Group of librarians acting as designated trainers. Policy and procedures manual (in-house). Regular information sheets and updates (in-house). Council IT section (technical support for communication lines, kilostream, and non DS equipment).
Fife	All in-house to library service at present limited by own knowledge. Beginning to be able to use IT specialist support now we are part of a bigger organization.

Authority	Management and training arrangements
Flintshire	1 computer systems librarian. Technical support from specialist unit in directorate.
Gateshead	1 IT projects officer with skills in Web editing, multimedia, desktop publishing etc. 2 Close liaison with Gateshead council's computer services department. 3 All reference library staff are trained and familiar with modern applications of information technology.
Glasgow	1 Specialist staff 2 In-house training 3 Training within city council 4 External courses 5 Departmental user groups.
Gloucestershire	Technical staff: systems development officer X 1; library systems supervisor X 1; PC support officers X 2; clerical assistant X 1. Public information system staff: electronic information manager X 1, clerical assistant X 2, Web designer temporary 6 month secondment. Training and awareness: partly delivered in-house and partly by FM company. Priorities are Windows/computer awareness and training to support applications/services available to public.
Greenwich	2 staff trained in Dynix systems administration. Liaise with communications/local hardware firms for support in these areas. Central hardware support through Ameritech/Bull Staff trained in-house on Dynix system.
Gwynedd	Ongoing training Re: BLCMP TALIS and as development of Internet network within authority.
Hackney	System support unit consist of two staff members. Use made of Council in-house IT unit when it can be afforded and external training.
Hammersmith/Fulham	Current library management system is run by library staff. New library system will be run by information technology services department as part of the corporate network.
Haringey	Systems manager. Open learning project officer. Open learning centre providing general computer training for all library staff and others.
Harrow	1 systems administrator. Support from senior cataloguer and support for day to day running of system server from IT dept's staff.
Hartlepool	At the moment we are relying heavily on external training courses and help from IT staff for help/technical expertise and training. With implementation of new system hope to appoint a project manager for fixed term as part of SCA funding to provide management/training initiative in-house.
Havering	Daily management by principal librarian technical services (librarian not IT specialist). Supported by Help desks at SBS and council IT services. Training done by SBS or onsite by branch librarians. Newsletter to keep staff up to date.
Hereford and Worcester	3 IT staff for TALIS. 1 staff for LOIS. All staff trained at implementation of TALIS.
Hertfordshire	Head of IT. IT Support officer. ALS Automation officer. 5 X IT service support specialists. PC – external. ALS Training – internal. CD-ROM packages and Internet – internal. Online searching – internal.
Highland	Partnership library/IS/BLCMP. Systems section (4 professional) but this covers multitude of systems including non IT.
Hillingdon	Library service is part of community services – it has an IT team of 4 covering IT in libraries, youth and recreation services. Management of the GEAC system, administration of the LAN in central library, support of users generally, production of management information.
Hounslow	1 Internet exploration project by information staff. 2 IT manager and his team (Network manager), Library system manager and assistants provide technical support.
Isle of Wight	Support from central IT department of council. Staff training in-house 'hands on'.
Islington	1 Technical management centralized within corporate IT dept. But they currently fund a systems manager post based within libraries to manage TALIS on a daily basis. An IT service manager is based in each directorate to negotiate and coordinate corporate IT resources for departments. 2 IT dept provides courses for standard word-processing packages. For all other IT training directorates bid on an annual basis for devolved budget. This budget used for external courses or commissioned training. 3 TALIS training: network of core trainers throughout the service who cascade train all staff. 4 Regular staff meetings and bulletins include IT updates. 5 Staff use CBT packages in our open learning centres on their closed days.

Authority	Management and training arrangements
Kensington and Chelsea	Computer services librarian. Oversees the management, development and training for the Dynix library management system and some council machines. She also ensures staff awareness of new developments. The council's IT contractors (DCS) manage and troubleshoot other departmental IT equipment. Input/Output provide and manage their own service and equipment.
Kent	4.5 FTE staff in the department and SLAs for other expertise. Minicomputer operated by FM company. Staff training is an ongoing process with a mixture on internal and external courses. Courses are usually run on demand, or when new hardware or software is delivered.
Kingston upon Thames	1 Technical management by system manager + one 18hr assistant 2 Training via key trainers – we have Investors In People award. 3 'connections' – staff newsletter produced every month. 4 Digital link to BLCMP very useful for system maintenance upgrades.
Kirklees	All arrangement and training by IT DSO
Knowsley	Network manager- computer specialist. Network technician – Librarian who is library management system specialist. Staff training and awareness given as new technologies are brought onto the library service.
Lambeth	Day to day running of system, and long term development is managed by library systems manager and systems officer in conjunction with BLCMP library services. Systems management comes within the libraries' client unit. Daily backup procedure and network management is carried out by Lambeth IT of the council's IT service. A system of key trainers is in operation for training in operation. A user group exists to promote staff awareness. Information/ awareness also dealt with through management and the libraries client newsletter.
Lancashire	The county library IT services system has 9 specialist IT staff in support supplies in LCL.
Leeds	Network supported by council IT staff. Internet Website for council in libraries (dedicated team). 1 manager, 1 database manager + 2 others. Systems support libraries – 2 staff. Staff training integrated into library training programme – under review.
Leicester	Specialist staff provided by Leicestershire Libraries as part of joint arrangement. Staff training done on an ad hoc basis.
Leicestershire	Management – TALIS: Libraries information systems team – part of the county council's information systems unit (ISU). Specialist support from other sections of ISU-network services. INFOLINX – Specialist team within libraries dept. Support from ISU. Internet – ISU. CD-ROM – Libraries information systems team – support ISU Training – Mixture of training provided by supplier of BLCMP for TALIS; external training agencies; in-house training – formal and informal. Awareness includes user groups and similar meetings, newsletters, periodicals; information on Intranet, contracts. Training for users in-house. For TALIS – dedicated training team during implementation, centralized formal training sessions for all staff in libraries using the system. Since then on-site plus centrally offered refresher/new staff sessions. Staff newsletters; departmental e-mail; in-house user group for procedural matters (used for both awareness and training) matters also brought to attention of senior staff as necessary.
Lewisham	CPU based in Town Hall (Capita Services) since Dec 1996. SLA for routine problem solving, support and hardware maintenance. Library Services still control management of the system.
Lincolnshire	All systems managed technically by staff of Lincolnshire council IT dept. In-house courses are arranged by the county council. No special arrangements for staff training and awareness. IT dept provide advice and support.
Liverpool	Libraries are part of leisure services directorate. Directorate computer services unit is responsible for network and hardware maintenance. Libraries system manager responsible for library housekeeping system and training. Libraries IT development officer responsible for leading on development of IT applications and related systems.
Luton	Joint arrangement with Beds CC until 1999 for Galaxy 2000. The library computer team provide training and technical support. For CD-ROM and Internet we have a contract with a special IT unit within the county council for maintenance and technological support. Training courses offered. Also working with IT in Luton borough for new equipment coming in.
Manchester	Manchester's automated library system (Galaxy 2000) is managed by three members of staff. These staff are also responsible for a wide variety of other tasks including computer training, installing software, running a departmental help desk service, software programming and hardware installations.
Merthyr Tydfil	Support from county council IT dept. General training.

Authority	Management and training arrangements
Merton	Currently one computer systems librarian. Departmental reorganization by 1 August 1997 will result in change of designation of this post to Business Systems Administrator reporting to departmental Business Systems Manager. Staff training on libraries' computer systems is offered on a needs basis and fitted in between other tasks.
Middlesborough	Technical management – IT dept. Staff training – as and when it is needed.
Midlothian	Technical and support staff receiving specialist training, e.g. Internet, MS Access, also HTML. Technical PC support from IT department. All professional; staff and appropriate assistant staff receiving introductory/intermediate PC/Internet /CD-ROM training from external training providers.
Milton Keynes	Access to MKC IT unit. Access to Bucks County on joint arrangements. Access to ALS support.
Monmouthshire	Free access to Internet 3 months before public launch. Windows 95 training for all staff. Use of Winlock software for security.
Moray	Computer section deal with technical aspects, ongoing applications and training for library staff.
Neath and Port Talbot	Liaison with the Authority's Education and IT staff. Library staff are commencing a detailed programme of IT training undertaken initially by internal specialists
Newcastle upon Tyne	Management and supervision is dispersed but overall responsibility lies with SSM and newly created post ICT Manager. Engineering support/maintenance – DS Ltd Software support/maintenance – DS Ltd. Comms – City IT (Network Manager) – DS Ltd and BT-SSM (support services management). Staff training/awareness – in-house training programme involves all draft. Detailed training documentation/ packages have been developed. Initial training from DS Ltd on implementation. Software development – strong commitment and dedicated staffing resources in-house, working with the company.
Newham	1 Technical manager; 1 Information Systems manager; 1 YT/Modern Apprentice. Staff attend training courses as appropriate, either in-house or external.
Newport	IT system librarian employed as LMS system librarian. Also responsible for supporting PC technology used for open learning services/CD-ROM databases in turn supported by council IT section for PC technology.
N.I. Belfast	DS systems engineer. 2 staff with specialist IT responsibilities. Formal training arranged in-house as required.
N.I. North Eastern	In-house IT manager. Specialist training given by BLCMP, trainers are trained and these trainers cascade training locally.
N.I. South Eastern	1 Systems Librarian and Systems support Librarian. Support and develop all existing IT and offer training in most areas. 2 Regional training Unit through FE Colleges. Offers standard WP, spreadsheet and database courses. 3 Special Development courses were offered for Internet. 4 As part of an Education Board we get assistance from Board's Computing and Training Staff.
N.I. Southern	System is provided on agenda basis by BCCCS. They provide training, technical and software staff as part of the agreement. Library has two staff for first approach on faults staff training is provided mainly by own staff, board staff, BCCCS staff and staff in local colleges of further education.
N.I. Western	Technical advice and staff training undertaken by Board's computer development officer and his section.
Norfolk	Assistant computer services officer. 1 FTE database assistant. System centre and communications maintained and supported by county council computer dept. A Technology Change panel consisting of all level staff has been set up to spearhead awareness of the issues and guide the training project. All new staff have 4 day training course in library management system, and a short session in the IT dept during 1 day library action course. Those using PCs for word-processing have half day 1 to 1 session. Staff at Norwich reference using CD-ROM network have short 2 to 1 training session on new products and time then allowed to practise with questions. Technology change days – a one-day awareness day for all staff in county on new IT developments to be completed by the end of 1997. Other occasional courses for all levels of staff as necessary.
North East Lincolnshire	ALS in partnership with 3 other authorities. PCS – authority wide in-house support. Training – in-house and external courses.

Authority	Management and training arrangements
North Lincolnshire	Technical Management – There are currently no specialist IT personnel in libraries and so only limited in-house management is done. Departmental and corporate IT depts are used for IT support. Some equipment also runs under maintenance agreements. Training and awareness – mainly in-house training as new services and software are introduced. There are some opportunities for staff to go on organised IT training (for basic IT skills) arranged corporately.
North Somerset	The Economic Development and Community Leisure Directorate has a systems manager responsible for all IT apart from library management system. Library management systems are the responsibility of a joint arrangement with Bristol City Council. Staff training etc. is the responsibility of the library information and support officer.
North Tyneside	Support services manager has overall responsibility for IT in libraries. An IT technician has been appointed to look after IT equipment, develop systems and train staff.
Northamptonshire	Management – libraries staff and NCC's IT services personnel. Training – mixture of in-house and external training necessary.
Nottinghamshire	1 Library systems team (3) run and maintain library management application (Book plus), with operational support and maintenance from authority IT dept. Systems team responsible for training and development, awareness etc. 2 Other PC-based h/w and applications (inc. Internet) maintained by IT Dept or by separate locally organized arrangements (e.g. for CD-ROM). Some training provided by IT Dept, otherwise ad hoc within library service.
Oldham	Systems manager (post frozen).
Orkney	Occasional training allowed at meetings when money available. Most help is given by phone and a member of staff here. (Phone the maintenance people). Staff training given for new updates given regularly.
Oxfordshire	IT section for department of Leisure and Arts 3.5 FTE. IT Manager – strategy, development etc Senior Asst IT Manager – library system management and administration, security, data protection, disaster planning, projects, management information. Assistant IT Manager – office automation, e-mail Internet etc, projects. (O.5 FTE) Assistant IT Manager – library system user group, training, testing, software development. All posts include training, current awareness, communications brief.
Pembrokeshire	The authority has (in theory!) a corporate approach to IT with training provided by (corporate training) – doesn't work too well. We keep trying to get a systems Librarian but have failed so far – this is what we desperately need.
Perth and Kinross	Technical training carried out by IT staff within council.
Poole	We still currently rely on Dorset, but via our own IT unit.
Portsmouth	PCC – Information Services Unit. DS Ltd. – engineers. Courses run by ISU.
Redbridge	1 full time library systems manager who works for the corporate information systems service. 18 hour post currently being filled on a temporary basis.
Redcar and Cleveland	All systems managed by specialist IT staff in liaison with resource service officer. Training is in-house by RSO. However, a new system is due for implementation Jan 1998. Full staff training programme for all staff is under development, involving training of key personnel by suppliers and cascaded to all other staff. Training to be in conjunction with data testing/ installation so that staff are able to get immediate hands on experience with no time lag between training and use of system.
Renfrewshire	All IT hardware and software in Renfrewshire Libraries is supported by the leisure services department, automated systems unit. This unit has 5 full time staff with leisure backgrounds. Currently 3 of the 5 have library backgrounds. This unit also oversees training for IT on corporate systems.
Rhondda	Technical management and support is carried out by the IT staff or Rhondda Cynon Taff County Borough Libraries based at Bronwydd House in Porth. In addition there is an IT assistant for libraries based at Treorchy library, Treorchy. Day-to-day training of staff is carried out in the workplace by the IT assistant. New developments would be explained and demonstrated to key staff at Bronwydd House in their training suite.
Richmond	The library management system is managed by a facilities management group (CFM) at an external site. There are no specialist systems staff on the library staff establishment. The post of IT Manager was created in April 1997. The role of the IT Manager is to maintain and develop current library IT applications as well as a strategic role. Most IT training is done in-house.

Appendix 5.1 Management and training arrangements.

Authority	Management and training arrangements
Rochdale	Systems manager responsible for ongoing technical management – advising on strategic IT issues, development programmes and implementation and training/support. Structure training and awareness sessions programmed into development plans involving appropriate staff and senior managers. 'Blue skies' awareness tends to be ad hoc and informal – limited number of staff and time preclude structuring this sort of work. Systems manager reports directly to Bibliographic and Special Services Librarian who takes overall responsibility for IT developments and budgets.
Rotherham	Technical support provided by supplies, e.g. ALS, Abacus + in-house from Council Information systems unit. Information system both manual + electronic, along with automated circulation system managed by principal librarian, Information services. Regular IT meetings held. Staff training + awareness managed largely in-house. Regional developments are in-hand South Yorkshire Network. Senior management very committed to EPI as essential part of service.
Rutland	Systems management is provided by Leicestershire. Local staff training as required.
Salford	IT services manager. Training courses for staff at open learning centre.
Sandwell	Library staff – Database manager (responsibility for system). Library support services manager plans for IT awareness to become 'core course' i.e. all staff must attend. Expected late 1997.
Scottish Borders	IT staff at HQ, also Specialist Business Solutions.
Sefton	Computer services librarian scale (full time) [a chartered librarian with computer knowledge]; Computer assistants X 2. Training is delivered:: (a) in-house by the above staff; (b) in-house by DS Ltd staff; (c) externally by the Council's central training unit, IT section specialist trainers.
Sheffield	Management of systems 1 Senior librarian with core responsibility for integrated library system management. 2 Systems technicians with responsibility for all leisure hardware maintenance, including integrated library system. All library staff received 5 days training in operation of library management system. Currently 1 FTE member of staff with responsibility for delivery of training on library management system. Other IT training covered from within overall department training budget.
Shropshire	In-house training for all staff, regular and ongoing as IT develops. One part time support officer.
Solihull	IT POINT is managed by specialist staff who also give advice on IT issues to other staff. All staff have visited IT POINT for awareness session. As IT is expanded relevant training is provided by internal and external trainers as appropriate. The manager of IT POINT also works for the Authority's IT services dept. and is available to upgrade skills valuable to the division.
Somerset	Principal assistant county librarian is responsible for strategic management and development of IT. Systems manager is responsible for technical management of systems. A one-day course on current IT developments will be run twice this year for members of staff at all levels. General systems training is carried out on an informal basis. Structured training is all staff planned when new system is implemented in 1998.
South Ayrshire	IT coordinator employed to develop cybercentres. It is planned to use in-house training which has been used with a fair level of success.
South Gloucestershire	The standalone IT is supported by staff from the IT unit within the authority. The library circulation system is supported by a team of staff from a neighbouring authority and also if required by BLCMP specialists.
South Tyneside	Systems librarian responsible for management training and development.
Southampton	1 DS Galaxy 200-run under SLA from Hampshire County Council maintained by part-time systems librarian 2 IT support from Southampton City Council IT section 3 IT Librarian – IT liaison officer 4 Staff training currently on demand.
Southwark	Full time IT manager and IT officer managing all IT throughout the service. Staff training is seen as important but is also difficult to manage. All professional staff were given 1 day Windows update winter 1996. All staff will receive 4 hours CD-ROM training during 1997. All staff will receive community information training in 1997 but details not yet finalized, for some staff this will include Internet training.
Staffordshire	GEAC Plus library management system run by county council computer centre staff with SLA. Some GEAC training for upgrades etc. Other IT Training arranged by county council IT section or independent trainers, LA courses etc. Electronic information support and training from Abacus software Ltd.

Authority	Management and training arrangements
Stirling	Dynix system run by operations librarian. Technical assistance from information services. Training supplied on ad hoc basis; mixture of self identification of needs and placement by arrangement.
Stockport	1 FTE systems librarian.
Stockton	IT project coordinator. Team of IT trainers. Dedicated IT training room. Regular user groups and newsletters. Liaison with and support from IT division.
Stoke on Trent	Staffing: IT officer. Part time assistant to be appointed. As a new library authority, we are in the process of establishing policies, so it is too early to comment in detail.
Suffolk	Staffing of system centre currently under review. Currently 3FT, 1PT. Training 3 day course for basic Galaxy 2000 – all staff organized centrally. Follow-up/refresher courses arranged locally. Galaxy 2000 handbook for staff support. 1 day CALM basic course. CALM 2000 handbook. Follow-up/refresher/advanced arranged locally. System centre staff trained by DS Ltd and attend external programmes. Windows and Internet courses both provided in-house and attended externally. Word 6 courses provided in-house and trainers brought in. Similar arrangements for CD-ROM, on live searching etc. Basically training and support managed by officer who is a member of Institute of Information Technology Trainers (MIITT). Training and support documentation provided for all hardware, software etc by a combination of in-house events, external programmes and open learning.
Surrey	1 DS Ltd. Surrey libraries have a seven year contract with DS Ltd. for the supply and maintenance of a library management system. All system management hardware and software support carried out by DS on the 300+ workstations and system centre, plus network. Help desk run by DS. Dedicated engineering based in Surrey. 2 Support for existing Internet, CD-ROM and learning centre workstations conducted by IS3 (internal SCC IT unit.) No library systems team. Some technical officers and trainers based with the 5 library areas. strategic IT developments and DS contract monitoring in-house.
Sutton	Use of Input/Output and internal/external courses.
Swansea	Technical staff supplied by corporate body. Training in systems operation assessed and implemented on an ongoing basis.
Swindon	Managed by borough council IT manager. Working with WCC IT management. Until termination of the lease in 1998.
Tameside	Principal officer (Bibliographic Services) is responsible for management of the system with the day to day operational management by system administrative + 2 part time operators for evening and Saturday cover. Additional support given by IT department. Training in IT matters is ongoing part of the IT programme.
Torfaen	All staff are encouraged to use the Internet and training in its use is regularly scheduled throughout the year. The purchase of a new automated library system will lead to detailed training of all staff in the new system.
Tower Hamlets	DS Galaxy run by Bib Services staff, 0 separately designated systems staff.
Trafford	No formal arrangements at the time of writing.
Upper Norwood	As part of installation of Heritage.
Vale of Glamorgan	1 principal librarian with responsibility for IT along with many other things. 1 IT officer. IT officer provides training to staff.
Wakefield	Currently under review.
Walsall	1 System management the responsibility of the library's support services manager 2 Current training arranged on a needs basis combination of in-house/external
Waltham Forest	IT systems development manager and 2 computer systems officer manage the library management system, CD-ROM, Internet, and PC developments in the arts and leisure department.
Wandsworth	DS Galaxy system managed by contractor (DSO from previous library computer staff.)
Warwickshire	Systems Librarian (IT Manager), operational support undertaken by County Council computing Dept
West Lothian	We have a F/T System Administrator fully trained on Dynix/Unix selected training on PC applications. All appropriate staff are given detailed training on new Dynix software releases. System Administrator train staff on basic PC applications.
West Sussex	We have no specialist IT staff. Developments are managed by Bibliographic staff and senior management staff working closely with the local authority IT staff who have detailed knowledge of library systems. The library service is responsible for the inter-departmental information management group coordinating the gathering and dissemination of public information through the county's Website.

Authority	Management and training arrangements
Westminster	Technical management of systems: 1 full time library systems manager; 1 full time senior systems assistant; 1 half time systems assistant. Also newly appointed information development librarian responsible for development of information through technology as opposed to GEAC system.
Wigan	IT support officer for leisure services recently appointed – looks after libraries as part of this brief. Training project basis, with launch, or with identified training needs from staff development. Provided by IT support officer, bought in by Council Central training from consultancy or college or provided by central training directly.
Wiltshire	The Library Services team of four staff has recently been transferred to the County Council Corporate IT Unit. (A new policy decision!) The Library Service has an SLA with Corporate IT.
Wirral	Principal Librarian (Bibliographical Services) and Systems Manager are responsible for technical management. Staff are sent on computer awareness courses plus more specialist training as appropriate.
Wolverhampton	Information systems librarian. Technical officer.
Wrexham	Arranged through education directorates IT staff or with County Borough's Information systems dept. The library and information service has a total of 11 professional staff throughout the county none of whom are IT or systems staff.
York Libraries	Council IT dept + support from system suppliers. Training – IT training team (council); system suppliers; in-house.

Appendix 5.2
Authorities with IT strategies

Berkshire	Kingston upon Thames	Redbridge
Bristol	Kirklees	Redcar and Cleveland
Bromley	Lancashire	Rochdale
Cambridgeshire	Leicestershire	Rotherham
Camden	Lincolnshire	Salford
Conwy	Liverpool	Scottish Borders
Coventry	Manchester	Shropshire
Durham	Monmouthshire	Somerset
East Lothian	N.Ireland Southern	South Tyneside
Edinburgh	Neath and Port Talbot	Southampton
Essex	Newcastle upon Tyne	Swansea
Glasgow	Norfolk	Walsall
Gloucestershire	North East Lincolnshire	Warwickshire
Hertfordshire	North Lincolnshire	West Sussex
Hillingdon	Northamptonshire	Westminster
Islington	Northumberland	
Kensington and Chelsea	Nottinghamshire	
Kent	Oxfordshire	

Appendix 5.3
System development plans

Authority	System development plans
Aberdeenshire	Extension of TALIS to five other libraries. Provision for Internet in more libraries; finance and time permitting.
Angus	(a) Replacement of system centre with NT server. (b) Increase in networking on CD-ROM and PC units (c) Introduction of Internet service (d) Use of Internet facilities to make community resources more available.
Barnet	Replacing Geac GLIS with Geac PLUS by end of 1997. Planning Internet access to community information linked to corporate website. EDI for orders etc. planned for 1998.
Barnsley	Extension of PC availability and/or Internet to most branch libraries under grant funding by end of 1997/8. Subject to grant funding, these will support open learning, homework and family learning projects. CD ROM loan being investigated. Automated circulation/catalogue extension to cover special services & extra branch library subject to grant funding.
Bath and N.E. Somerset	End of current system December 1997.
Bedfordshire	Cybercafé at one library in conjunction with lifelong learning unit. Extension of Internet access.
Berkshire	More sites on Dynix library system.
Bexley	Preparation for Dynix upgrade during Easter 1998. Extension of Internet access for staff.
Birmingham	Delivery of EPIS via WW; cable access to Internet + multimedia CD-ROM across WAN in selected sites.
Bolton	Implementation of Inform – community information module on TALIS with access via Internet. Public Internet access. OPAC Web interface.
Bournemouth	Internet to reference library and senior management desk tops. Internet pilot project at one library (5 PCs installed and managed in conjunction with commercial partner).
Bradford	Homework centre for central library.
Brent	1 Extend Internet access to more service points 2 Online radio link for mobile service 3 Increase the number of CD-ROM terminals and PCs for online.
Bridgend	Introduce CD-ROM facilities to smaller branch libraries. Introduce open learning facilities to the central library and information library. Increase word-processing facilities. Introduce GEOPAC (Windows based OPAC) to replace present terminal OPACs.
Brighton and Hove	1 Capital challenge project – networking of all schools and libraries – access to Internet etc. in all public libraries. 2 New library computer system – due in Dec 1997 – will include community information and ability to interface with other systems. 3 Project to develop content for new network to publicise/promote libraries and museums service once new network in place. 4 Flexible learning project – new centre in BCT joint project with SRB funding – will lead to distance learning opportunities in public libraries.
Bromley	1 LAN technology in over 50% of Bromley libraries by March 1998. 2 A community information system based on Internet/intranet technology by March 1998 3 PC hire to 50% of libraries by Nov 1997.
Buckinghamshire	Access to the Internet for staff and public. Community information and catalogue available via the Internet. Extend CD-ROM network to more branches.
Bury	Internet public access (July 1997). Completion of authorized circulation and catalogue system to further 4 libraries. Expansion of open learning service

Authority	System development plans
Caerphilly	1 Multimedia – (CD-ROM reference) to 13 libraries including separate provision for youth in 4 libraries 2 Public access to Internet extending to 4 libraries 3 PC for public hire in 1 library 4 Community information via library management system available through OPACs 5 Public access OPACs in every static service point
Calderdale	Internet access to be via a megastream link, rather than dial-up.
Cambridgeshire	Extension of library automation system to 6 more libraries. Completion of programme to convert all existing network links from X25 to router. Installation of OPACS into 2 more libraries. Extension of public access to electronic public information system to 5 more libraries. Extension of Internet access to 2 more libraries and central stock unit. Extension of public GIS access to 1 more library. Wide area CD-ROM networking to 4 key referral libraries. Internet access to library catalogue. Introduction of EDI with library suppliers. Major upgrade to DYNIX software. Replace dumb terminals on electronic public information points with Internet – linked PCs.
Camden	Public Internet access at three of four sites and further networking of CD-ROM through libraries.
Ceredigion	Money is available under regional challenge 5b area status for rural areas and it is intended to use this to extend our computer issue system to the smaller p/t branches and provide access to electronic information hopefully Internet access in 4 branches.
Cheshire	Extend library management system network. Extend OPACs. Extend Internet access.
City of London	Replacement library system hosting an Internet site.
Conwy	1 2nd public Internet access point established (and possibly 3rd) 2 Public Internet familiarization sessions 3 Community information to be fully computerized 4 Website managed by LIS other Borough Council site or in partnership with private company, Gaia communications to manage virtual Llandudo site. 5 TNA to identify staff training and development needs re IT.
Cornwall	Internet access to public in larger libraries if pilot goes well, also word-processing facilities.
Croydon	Acquisitions using EDI to all major suppliers. Redesign of OPAC screens. Borrower self-enquiry and self-issue. Extension and development of Croydon Online. Public e-mail extended and all libraries connected to CD-ROM network.
Cumbria	Access points to Cumbria's Genesis lifelong learning and information system through 6 libraries.
Darlington	OPAC –To include community information.
Denbighshire	1 Investigation into upgrading/replacing the Galaxy Management system. 2 Extending the Internet facility to all libraries in conjuction with the local TEC.
Derby	EDI for stock ordering.
Derbyshire	EDI for stock ordering.
Devon	Upgrade of the library management system to GALAXY 2000.
Doncaster	(a) Continuation of computerization project – some branches not yet added to system – awaiting decision on budget cuts. Some planned installations may be closing. (b) Progress towards greater use of CD-ROMs at branch library level (c) Catalogue soon to be loaded on to Unity to facilitate ILL (d) Plan to tender for replacement to GEAC early 1998
Dorset	1 Completing computerization of all service points. 2. Moving community information to new Internet compatible platform.
Dundee	The City-wide electronic information network will be upgraded during 1997–8 to include Internet access at all points and an increase in the number of locations.
Durham	We have a bid for Rechar funding (EROF) to put public access PCs in all libraries in the east of the County.
Ealing	Current plans to upgrade the library network to support TCP/IP and to install a CD-ROM server. We hope to use the upgraded network to access the CD-ROM server and the intranet/Internet. Ealing is developing a corporate intranet site which will be linked to the community Information database.
East Ayrshire	No concrete plans for implementation this year.
East Dumbartonshire	Access to library catalogue via Internet. CD-ROM lending. Internet strategy.
East Lothian	Council information strategy to be launched. Community information supplied to council/public in database form. Possible establishment of branch circulations extension of PC provision in branches

Authority	System development plans
East Renfrew	Alongside our IT division it is hoped to be move to public access terminals by July 1997. This pilot project is being funded by the IT division, but it is also part of the decentralization strategy of the council. It will take 15–18 months to do all our sites. Online for the library management system.
East Riding	Goole IT centre.
East Sussex	The current rental agreement for our McDonnell Douglas system expires at the end of 1997. We are currently in the tendering process for a replacement system to go live in January 1998. This development overshadows everything at the moment.
Edinburgh	Public Access Internet projects in the central reference and Craigmillar libraries will be reviewed in 1998. They have been trialled on a free basis and decisions on future charging policies will be made. PC and CD-ROM facilities in community libraries will be expanded during 1997–8. The outcome for a bid for a new integrated computer system should be known by the end of 1997–8. The new Wester Hailes library will have Edinburgh's first Youth library offering a range of IT facilities for young people. A relational database (remote access) is being developed for the 'cap-info' system.
Enfield	Continuing development of Enfield Website.
Essex	Replacing library system with GEAC plus. Training 700 + staff; dramatically increasing OPACs.
Fife	Increase Internet access for public, enable Internet access for senior management.
Flintshire	Website part of corporate initiative. Public access Internet. Decision on new library management system. Corporate intranet – pilot in progress.
Gateshead	Gateshead Council's Libraries and Arts service is the key coordinator of the North of England regional information service, a pilot project of Northern Informatics. Several technical developments will be implemented by the end of 1997/8 including installation of a regional search enquire and stage 1 of the regional intranet. By September 1997 Gateshead Council's WWW site will be live. The EC funded Reactive Telecom project will be completed in June 1997. By then, voice recognition will be intergrated in to the cable TV information service.
Glasgow	Cooperating with 10 Glasgow FE colleges which are networked as Glasgow telecollege network.
Gloucestershire	1 Replacement of existing library management system – migration to BLCMP Talis system in progress – will be complete by March 1998. 2. Upgrades of corporate network to 15 additional libraries to support Internet access to public information system – Glosnet. 3 Full public access to Internet probably in 6 libraries. 4 Networking CD-ROMs to a further 4 libraries. 5 E-mail connectivity project to staff in group offices.
Greenwich	Public CD-ROM access. Corporately explore Internet access staff/public
Gwynedd	Further expansion of system to other libraries and upgrade of system to Talisweb. Also hope to provide CDROM facilities in 6 other libraries.
Hammersmith/Fulham	1 Trial of public access to information held on CD–ROM at one of the reference libraries to take place late August. 2. Replacement library management system to be installed before March 1998 3 Pilot project of intranet/Internet access to council and community information being undertaken as part of corporate strategy.
Hampshire	Introduction of OPACs.
Haringey	Introduction of TALIS to replace and upgrade existing system – Autumn 1997. Networking of library system with main council network. Also to link up with one-stop shops/leisure line etc. January 1998 introduction of INFORM for community information. Future link up to Internet. Third open learning centre due to open November 1997 then standalone PC packages at branches.
Harrow	All branches fully automated for circulation. Community information module fully implemented.
Hartlepool	We are currently out to tender for a replacement automated library system. We have gained SLA for above project and are looking for a system that will provide us with full range of automated services including OPAC/community information/mobile-B Bus Online as well as full circulation/acquisitions package. Hope to be 'online' with circulation by Dec/Jan 1998 with the rest to follow later in 1998.
Havering	Community information system supplied by SBS based on networked multimedia PCs.
Hereford and Worcester	Internet via County council site.
Hertfordshire	CD-ROM/word-processing/ Internet access for all libraries.
Highland	Additional sites automated (total up to 35). Community information automated. Internet access. Dedicated OPACs for the public.

Authority	System development plans
Hillingdon	Exploring networking of CD-ROMs, but plans not yet concrete.
Hounslow	CD-ROM network at 3 main libraries.
Isle of Wight	1 further library online for circulation.
Islington	1 Public Internet service to be extended to a number of libraries by March 1998. 2 CD-ROM network for public and staff to be operational in central library by March 1998.
Kensington and Chelsea	We have plans for public Internet access + CD-ROM networking for financial years 1998–9 and 1999–2000.
Kent	We are currently out to tender for a complete replacement system. Implementation will start in 1997–8, all service points will be automated if resources allow.
Kingston upon Hull	Business network. Community information network.
Kingston upon Thames	1 Internet access in all service points using 2 Mb leased lines to borough Web server (http://www.kingston.gov.uk) – at least 9 public Internet PCs not including new Tolworth library. 2. Staff trained in use of Internet and offer assistance to public. 3 Access to Web server (intranet) is free – browsing on WWW remains charged.
Kirklees	1 Public access word-processing at 6 main libraries in July. 2 Public access Internet at 6 main libraries by December. 3 LIBRIS OPAC and EPIC at 6 libraries by early summer. 4 Lottery funded digital imaging system implemented by summer. 5 Contract award for new automated library system, January 1998. 6 Offline standalone PCs for Libris EPIC Web site not yet accessible through local authority outlets. 7 Kirlees information points being developed during this year. Libraries involved in planning. Access will be via kiosks.
Knowsley	Dynix library management system will be upgraded to Bull Escala 152 in autumn 1997. Kirkby library will have 29 machines linked to a local area network. Alyton library will have 40 machines linked to a local area network. Page Moss library will have 20 machines linked to a LAN. 100 new CD-ROMs are now being introduced to libraries.
Lancashire	Major system replacement process underway.
Leeds	Additional sites online – expect 7. Public access to Internet. 1 additional open learning centre. Possible/probable SRB bid for 'online@leeds' – 4 sites.
Leicester	City Council Website. Opening of Input/Output centre.
Lewisham	Public Internet access in all libraries.
Lincolnshire	A commitment to having e-mail at a minimum of one terminal for each of 6 areas – mainly for staff use/communication in first instance.
Liverpool	• Upgrading BLS to TALIS. • Public Internet access at a number of community libraries. • Telecentre in central library. • Automated community information system.
Luton	Increase the provision of CD-ROM PCs at the larger branches. Put the Internet into 2 largest libraries. OPACs into the central library. Create an IT area in the reference/business library with word-processing facilities.
Manchester	• Extending no. of OPAC terminals in district libraries with access to Manchester's catalogue and various CD-ROM databases. • Installing automated library system in Manchester prison. • Introducing departmental intranet. • Extending IT centres to more libraries. • Taking lead role in development of City-wide intranet service.
Merthyr Tydfil	1 Public Internet access 2 Computer suite with 4 new machines at the central library. CD-ROM/open learning uses. Served by network connections.
Merton	• Introduction of CD-ROM to reference and information service • Internet access by end of year • Dial-in access to Merton Local Information Network(Merlin).
Middlesbrough	1 Two pilot public information kiosks should be in place in libraries by the end of 1997 2 We are currently out to tender for a new library system, to be implemented by 1 April 1998
Midlothian	Three libraries – public access PCs for word-processing, catalogue, local information, CD-ROM One library – Internet plus training for public use.
Milton Keynes	An Input /Output centre, PC with Internet access at one library(possibly)

Authority	System development plans
Monmouthshire	Internet/CD-ROM/ PC for hire in 4 libraries. CD-ROM network, possibly county wide. CD-ROM in 5 libraries. Fax in all libraries. Replacement library management system before December1997. Mobile computerization by March 1998. Authority WAN.
Neath and Port Talbot	Extend PC availability to 14 of the larger libraries. New mobile library will have IT facilities. Internet access to at least one other library. We are currently reviewing our existing computer management system and reviewing alternative companies.
Newcastle upon Tyne	EDI for orders/reports and invoices with intention to include payment at the earliest opportunity. NLIS are taking the lead in developing EDI at a corporate level. Inter-library loans via Internet and Artel Community computer facilities – ongoing. Provision of multimedia resources for children and young people – formulating a strategy for implementation 1998–9. SRB One-stop shop development. EU projects: Equality – electronic services to the disadvantaged including housebound readers (in progress). Distinct – developing smart-card technology with a wide variety of applications, commencing January 1998. Promise – a virtual museum project. Communications network upgrade to enable networked multimedia applications for public access. CD-ROM network extension to all library sites. Developing Web page front end and enabling access to the library system via the authority's intranet. Drawing up specification for serials management system.
Newham	All libraries connected to the Council network, which will provide access to Internet and intranet services. New open learning centre in Beckton Library in April 1998 – six PCs.
N.I. Belfast	Computer suite networked facilities – under consideration.
N.I. North Eastern	Internet access to be provided for staff at 4 additional sites by Jan 1998. Circulation network to 10 libraries by April 1998. Public access to the Internet by Jan 1998. Additional CD-ROM PCs in 4 childrens libraries. 1 new open learning centre in 1997–8.
N.I. South Eastern	1 Hope to extend online circulation to another service point. 2 Hope to install 2 more public access CD-ROM PCs (in each of 2 service points) 3 Hope to give public access to Internet in 2 where only staff access now.
N.I. Southern	More libraries added to online system
N.I. Western	1 Extension of LANs 2. Use of dial-up to access online (real time) system.
Norfolk	Internet access for a further 7 service points for staff use. We are in the process of tendering for a new library management system. Replace postal ILL requests by e-mail.
North East Lincolnshire	Completion of network developments – WAN and LAN. These network developments will allow completion of the CD-ROM network within the central library and the business development link for the regional ERDF funded business network. Extension of Internet and e-mail facility within the library service. CD-ROM loan service. Network developments in support of an open learning project. Extension of the OPACs.
North Lincolnshire	Digital mapping to be introduced into 3 largest service points in North Lincolnshire. Networking of bibliographic tools (from system centre in Hull) to Scunthorpe central library. Networking of business information resources from Hull to Scunthorpe reference library (part of an ERDF funded project)
North Somerset	1 Joint library computer system currently out to tender. This involves Somerset county, N. Somerset council, S. Gloucestershire council and Bath and N.E. Somerset council in a joint exercise to produce a new library automation system. 2 Learning line – we are a partner in a bid to provide learning information, with WEST-EC and Learning Partnership West, with DfEE funding.
North Tyneside	Intend to have public Internet access in some form this year. Library system is now due for upgrade – process has started.
Northamptonshire	Development of county council public information service of which Northamptonshire Libraries and Information service is lead department, based on existing data available in computerized, viewdata and hardcopy form. Will ultimately be available in the Internet in at least 25 sites.
Northumberland	Informing Northumberland will provide broadband access to two libraries. (10 in total by 1999–2000). Potential applications include Internet, CD-ROM, distance learning, videoconferencing.
Nottinghamshire	1 Upgrade management system central processor (IBM AS/400) 2 Enquiry facilities on Book Plus to 9 more branches 3 Pilot offline circulation on 1 mobile library 4 Pilot public access Internet service at 2 sites 5 Pilot community information system 6 Feasibility study on network for all sites.

Authority	System development plans
Oldham	Pilot community information project – Internet-based made available in pilot centres via intranet.
Orkney	We should have CDROM facilities available for public use (adults and junior). PCs and Internet planned for future new library which will probably be 4/5 years.
Oxfordshire	OPAC terminals into all connected files. OPAC terminals (minimum offline) into next band of files. Offline staff enquiry/stock management faciilities most sites.
Pembrokeshire	Applied for slice of corporate IT funding to get more libraries online. ERDF funding available for access points in rural Wales – again corporate approach – struggle to convince them that libraries are natural access points for information! They prefer supermarkets!
Perth and Kinross	Replacement of existing BookshelF system 1997–98.
Poole	None. Longer term looking to reviewing the system we use and seeing whether an alternative would provide advantages.
Portsmouth	1 DS Galaxy 2000 – stand alone system Autumn/Winter 1997 2 Telecentres 3 CD-ROM – for loan 4 OPACs (as part of Galaxy 2000) 5 Internet (as part of PCC intranet) 6 Internet (public access)
Powys	The OPAC/Internet will be installed in all libraries by the end of 1998. Archives scanning project for key documents. Hope to produce a CD-ROM for schools. Records retrieval service for council currently using Powys network is planned to transfer onto WWW in 2 years or so.
Redcar and Cleveland	New library system will be implemented in all libraries by March 1998. All libraries will have aquisitions, circulation, enquiry, OPAC, Internet, Community information, MIS, Communications, borough council information system. Tender responses are due back in June 1997; with selection of a system due to be made at leisure and libraries sub committee in September 1997.
Renfrewshire	We will be moving from our current system to GEAC Plus run on a Sun processor over the summer with a live date of early October. This will allow us to get community information online and to use EDI for orders; we will also have the user capacity to implement OPACs which we don't now.
Rhondda	Unfortunately we are still operating two library systems with a third part of the authority not yet automated. Our chief priority therefore, is to extend the OLIB library management system to the entire library service and it is hoped to complete this process this year.
Richmond	1 Develop IT strategy document which will include: examining possible links with computer systems in adjacent authorities, CD-ROM networking, Internet access (public), conversion of community information to Internet delivery. 2 Produce implementation plan for computer system upgrade and identify sources of funding.
Rochdale	Addition of at least 2 (possibly 4) branches by April 1998 – circulation, OPAC, community information. Specialist OPACs – children's GUI OPAC at 5 sites; visually impaired OPAC at 4 sites. Replacement of Kurzweil and Brailler at one site and addition of text reader facilities at two others. Additional OPAC facilities at two sites. Expansion of use of and training for PCs at three sites (Staff). Additional OPACs at three sites. Two new open learning sites. Installation of Windows NT server for PC network – funding not yet agreed. Public access PC for cached Internet pages available from Jan/Feb 1998. (Part of Gracie Fields Centenary will include a Website). This will be an opportunity to get the links installed for Internet use. At first we will only be providing offline service to the public dependent on resources. Staff training access to the Internet – installation of links followed by programme of awareness and training; including building navigational tools etc. for the public. Work programme until 2000 includes additional 7 libraries online; enhanced stand alone CD-ROM facilities at one site.
Rotherham	1 Public access to Internet. 2 Implementation of acquisitions package. 3 Implementation of self-service functions in 4 service points. 4 Translation of videotext system into HTML to provide WWW access. 5 Launch of Electronic Community magazine using intranet. 6 Library and information services taking lead role in RMBC Website creation.
Rutland	Plans for public access PCs for use of CD-ROM, WP, Internet access. Will only come into fruition with possible partnership and sponsorship ventures.
Salford	Health information. Kiosk. Internet access to public. Specification for automation.

Authority	System development plans
Sandwell	Upgrade system to GENESIS. Move acquisition to EDI. CD-ROM PCs for all libraries. Better use of existing CD-ROM PCs – use for Internet. Experiment with network (moving from existing standalone narrow band to council wide band.)
Sheffield	Increase no. of Internet connections. In the next month all static service points will have OPAC terminals installed. Total number of OPAC terminals will be 108. Automated circulation will be introduced on all 5 mobile libraries. Inclusion of S. Yorkshire training access points database on public OPAC terminals.
Solihull	Have received funding from NIACE to provide 6 PCs for installation into homes for people with disabilities or those who are housebound. Initial and ongoing training is provided through telecollege and technical support provided by IT POINT.
Somerset	We are currently engaged in a tendering process for a new system. This is a joint project with 4 other local authorities, the aim being to have a shared bibliographic and community information database. The new system will automate all libraries, allowing the potential for CD-ROM networking and Internet access at all locations, plan remote access to databases.
South Ayrshire	New 5 station LAN for public access In a small rural library to be launched in August/September.
South Gloucestershire	S. Gloucestershire council is committed to automating all of its libraries. The programmes will commence in December 1997. Community Information will be incorporated into the council's one stop shops. Basic data about council services is currently being loaded for internal use. This will become publically available in the libraries as the hardware is provided. A collection of CD-ROMs for hire from Ramesis has been subscribed to and will be divided between the two libraries. CD-ROM equipment is currently being installed.
South Lanarkshire	Currently in the middle of 2 year project to integrate 4 library management systems by October 1998. Should have all static points online by end of 1997.
South Tyneside	Public access to Internet by Dec 1997. CD-ROMs for info:PCs installed in 2 branches and central children's by March 97. Acquisitions package purchased – full specification being worked on – live April 1998.
Southampton	Move towards an independent library system for city council by April 1998. Keeping links with local educational institutions and other local library services – beginning of implementation April 1998. OPAC 1998. All libraries online 1998. Business planning currently underway.
Southwark	1 CD-ROM networking – WAN between 2 major reference collections. LAN within branches where current use of standalone machines is significant. 2 Community Information will be published on WWW when council resolves firewalling issues. 3 E-mail using MS Exchange within libraries' senior management team.
Staffordshire	More libraries with automated circulation. OPACs in main libraries. PCs in most libraries with Internet access Plus, Internet, Electronic information – step in and financial information on mainframe. Corporate strategy to move to Windows 95 and Microsoft Office 97 will be implemented in admin areas.
Stirling	Council wide intranet in under development – not yet scheduled for libraries.
Stockton	Currently in the process of implementing Talis web OPAC; Talis web inform; Internet access; public access terminals.
Stoke on Trent	1 OPAC public access – pilot project. 2 Community information – extension to all service points, probably networked to online libraries – extending public access. 3 Internet access for staff at online libraries. 4CD-ROM Network pilot project.
Suffolk	Web catalogue – June 1997; community information on Web – end of 1997. Roll out of Web to all 41 libraries – end of 1997. Office automation over WAN e-mail to all libraries, March 1998.
Sunderland	Not able to say anything concrete at this stage, ambition is to extend public access to PC based systems and Internet.
Surrey	1 Networked CD-ROMs on staff and public terminals 2 Internet access via public terminals across library system network 3 Linking of library system network with SCC corporate network, providing wide access to intranet, other SCC departments., cc:mail etc. 4 Remote access to library system via laptop in mobile libraries etc. 5 EDI 6 Access to catalogue/community info via the Internet.
Sutton	Additional public access on CD-ROM PCs.

Authority	System development plans
Swansea	Plan to extend automation to all locations. Expand Internet provision and establish our intranet presence.
Swindon	Preparation of spec for new library computer system, including tender and issue of order.
Tameside	Anticipate selecting and training implementation of new system.
Torfaen	Internet access in all libraries probably via the new OPACs and the council's own Internet server.
Trafford	Introduction of BLCMP TALIS system into our libraries starting this financial year.
Upper Norwood	Looking for sponsorship for 2 PC's for public use and in particular for homework.
Walsall	Aim to link all district libraries to the Internet and provide multimedia facilities by March 1998. This will be supported by an upgrade in the library network at each site, to provide a minimum 128 Kbs link to the system centre/council Internet.
Waltham Forest	Completion of library system transfer from MDIS to Ameritech. Public access to the Internet through most if not all libraries. Further CD-ROM networking.
Wandsworth	Tender to replace/upgrade DS Galaxy in 1998–9. Internet access for public at refurbished Putney library (late autumn 1997)
Warwickshire	1 Introduce more Internet Centres in libraries. 2 Introduce more open learning centres in libraries. 3 Hope to develop and improve IT network (wide area) and introduce public information system.
West Lothian	First of the Internet access in libraries will be available by the end of 1997–8. We hope to have Web access to our catalogue around the same time.
West Sussex	1 Upgrading of acquisitions, cataloguing and circulation to a GALAXY 2000 system in 1997–8. 2 Moving to broadband network in 1998–9 which will permit expansion of networked services e.g: CD-ROM , Internet.
Westminster	• Staff access to Internet at all sites. • Extension of network to 2 more sites • Public Internet at at least 1 more site.
Wigan	• Public access to information strategy in development. • Replacement and expansion of circulation system to all branches with integrated system is being investigated.
Wiltshire	URICA system to be replaced during April–September 1998. Decisions on replacement system due end of June 1997. Library network to be replaced with the introduction of new system.
Wirral	BLCMP BLS system will be replaced by BLCMP TALIS in November 1997.
Wolverhampton	Public access to Internet. Increase CD-ROM network.
Wrexham	Currently upgrading to Galaxy 2000 and installing management systems at extra libraries.
York Libraries	OPACs should be in place in most service points by the end of 1997–8. Mobile library will be linked to Genesis.

Appendix 5.4
Final comments

Authority	Comments
Bexley	We are planning to develop an integrated strategy for IT development and management.
Bournemouth	New unitary authority from April 1997, therefore IT strategy not yet developed. Review of library management systems due in 1998–9. Review of community information system due in 1998–9.
Brighton and Hove	IT telematics strategy being drafted now will send copy once approved. Lots happening at the moment. Enormous potential to develop and transform services. Brief note about Capital Challenge project attached.
Buckinghamshire	There are a number of plans which we hope will take off this year in the new Bucks County Council, particularly working with partners on extending Internet access, community information, CD-ROM networks, Learning Line etc. Online searching has been overtaken by our large CD-ROM network which the public can access themselves.
Caerphilly	Strategy for library service including IT in preparation as part of overall departmental plan (community education, leisure and libraries).
City of London	Work is underway on our imaging project to capture and digitise 40,000 works in the corporations prints, maps, drawings and fine art collections. To be launched to the public in 1998/9.
Conwy	Unitary authority set up in April 96 and seriously hampered by small scale. Budget for whole library, information and Archive Service for 1997/98 £1,050,000 (after 11% county wide budget cuts). IT is considered a priority.
Darlington	As Darlington Borough Council only took over the library service on 1st April 1997 and we have had to implement a totally new IT system – and set up our bibliographic services department – and set up an inter-library loans services.
Dumfries and Galloway	Copy of IT strategy attached.
Durham County Council	In April 1997 the library's catalogue/ordering system moved from the IBM mainframe to a Unix system using an Oracle database.
East Ayrshire	East Ayrshire library and information services main objective is to merge the 2 library management systems which existed prior to reorganization. The lack of a single council wide system adversely affects staffing levels, service quality and development and the provision of management information.
East Dumbartonshire	We are presently working on an IT strategy in conjunction with council plans.
East Renfrew	We have agreed that when all our systems are up and running it will be our strategy to develop IT in as many areas as possible to the benefit of our customers/council.
East Riding of Yorkshire	IT strategies in preparation
Edinburgh	CAPINFO in the City of Edinburgh Council's Public information system, available in kiosks and free-standing PCs. It generates 73,000 enquiries a month over 54 sites. It will provide a flexible platform for other databases. The Internet, and local TV (channel 6). Developments taking place 1997–8.
Enfield	IT strategy being written. Subset of community information database and other information available on Website.
Flintshire County	New unitary – corporate IT culture slowly emerging. Many shared arrangements with neighbouring authorities are proving to be transient.
Gateshead	Gateshead is involved in several other areas of IT development. 1 In providing access to information for people with sensory impairments e.g., through Airs, information is transcribed into Braille, large print and audio through a variety of automated processes. Also the ELVIS project is providing video telephony access to libraries for deaf sign language users. 2 There is a track record in electronic multimedia publishing with CD-ROM and CD 3 Much development has occurred through involvement in European telematic projects.
Glasgow	IT and networking are the only way forward.

Authority	Comments
Gloucestershire	IT development is a key action for 1997–8 and will continue to be so in 1998–9. Libraries are managing the development of Glasnet – the corporate electronic information system.
Haringey	It is early days for us but this year, with the upgrade of TALIS, will I hope mark a real move towards a more IT-based service with a move towards public access to computers/information and eventually the Internet. Since their introduction this year the CD-ROMs have proved popular with children. Open Learning is thriving in the Borough at the moment. The computer centre is starting to be popular.
Hartlepool	Public access PCs: we currently have 1 of the above in use on The Headland which has been set up to provide access to Word/Windows as a community development project for unemployed – CV use etc. Hope to expand on this to other branches when we implement.
Highland	IT is regarded here only as a tool which we will use where appropriate to support service delivery. Naturally in such a rural area IT is crucial in compensating for deprivation of distance. Cost is always a drawback.
Kent County Council	The department is currently out to tender for a new system. Decision expected during the summer. Medway town becomes a unitary in April 1998. They will probably share our system for 2–3 years.
Kirklees	Current review of libraries by members is considering IT role in its widest context.
Knowsley	Knowsley MBC is currently undertaking a community information project to link a wide range of council buildings to the Internet and will be writing its own Web pages. These will include information about the libraries. Knowsley libraries have a WAN linking them to Knowsley community college with a text only facility.
Leicestershire	Library Management additional note: CD-ROM network currently under development. Network server installed + pilot at public service point due summer 1997. Networked CD-ROM on wide area network Local CD-ROM network for bibliographic databases for staff use at library HQ. CD-ROM facilities are also used by library services to education – a business unit within the county.
Lewisham	IT strategy in hand.
Lincolnshire	Getting central IT departments to understand the importance of public access to IT is proving to be more difficult than converting the Pope to paganism!
Liverpool	Send the next questionnaire on disk if possible!
Luton	We are just linking in with borough strategy and policy in regard to IT, an outline of needs up to 2001 is being worked on, to start develop an IT strategy. First details are enclosed but it is early days yet!
Midlothian	We are members of EARL and have nice home pages which are being developed to include a wider range of information. I had to say NO to many questions where I would really prefer to say YES – come back in a few months time!
Milton Keynes	Input/Output due soon (July). Internet community information being actively explored – intelligent villages project and other initiatives. IT strategy – corporate IT strategy under discussion. A library strategy is developing via committee reports linked to other local initiatives. Information will also be included in any library service plan.
Monmouthshire	Very daunting workload for a small service with few staff. Increasingly difficult for small authorities to keep up without strong corporate support.
Newcastle upon Tyne	(a) Electronic version of this please. (b) Expansions of the system to include: 1 Remote access from homes 2 Internet access to and from the library system 3 Interactive applications.
N.I. Belfast	Re acquisitions facilities – we use our catalogue to input items 'on order' and the report generator facility to print orders. We do not receipt material other than to remove the on order details when the item is received or to delete records for items on order which are either out of print or not supplied within the allotted time.
N.I. North Eastern	We are at an early stage of computerization, but having acquired our own system centre in April 1997 we have plans for rapid development. Prior to April 1997 we were hosted remotely on a data general computer at Queen's University Belfast.
N.I. South Eastern	Have experienced slashing cuts with minimal finance for expansion.
Norfolk	The majority of Internet access PCs are at county hall not at service points. These are used for networked office automation and corporate e-mail.
North East Lincolnshire	See attached brochure.

Authority	Comments
North Lincolnshire	There are other long term aims for IT strategy. These include the establishment of multimedia centre within Scunthorpe, the development of a community information network and the possibility of digitized photograph collections.
Northumberland	The issues of access/connection and tariffs are still major concerns for authorities such as this, where the market will not provide for rural areas. These questions need to be addressed as a national concern and not left to local resolution.
Nottinghamshire	1 'Enquiry only' access to library catalogue not represented in section 1. We have 15 small branches with access via ISDN line allowing enquiry, reservations, stock processing etc. Section II (2) = 9 more branches. 2 Local goverment reorganization will make a major difference to these responses after April 1998. Nottingham City will become a separate library authority with its own separate strategy and arrangements. Shared arrangements for the current library management system are expected for the medium term.
Oxfordshire	The attached strategy paper encompasses most of the points we would wish to make. Libraries face a real challenge over the next few years to be a vital part of the information society. Our department will continue to make strides to integrate access to resources across the whole of its functions (libraries, museums, archives, arts, countryside) and seek to use IT to promote and give access to these through all service points. The library has a distinct role as the gateway to the content of such collections.
Pembrokeshire	We are looking for some outside influence – Audit Commission, Welsh Office etc. – they may be able to influence funding. There are so many strands – Europe, LIP Wales etc. – risk that situation becomes confused and libraries fall between stools.
Poole	I am hopeful that the smaller unit of Poole Borough will achieve more in IT terms than the geographically widespread Dorset did, but obviously budgets are a limiting factor. The central library is at least soon to be linked to the civic centre, giving us (staff) e-mail and Internet access.
Redbridge	IT strategy in draft form only and not yet agreed by the management team.
Redcar and Cleveland	The libraries are currently in a state of transition; all borough systems are due to be withdrawn from the former county mainframe by March 1998. Therefore, the specification has been published and tender responses are awaited. Live libraries are due to migrate by the end of January 1998 and non-live libraries are to be added by March 1998.
Richmond	Service restructuring in April 1997 has changed management balance to allow IT issues to be fully addressed.
Rotherham	Use of IT to be led by information strategy, rather than technology leading service. Rotherham LIS is committed to the use of IT in delivering efficient and effective services. We are also keen to develop regional and authority wide partnerships where appropriate e.g. Rotherham's information superhighway strategy steering group.
Rutland	As a new authority Rutland has a lot of catching up to do and little budgetary provision in this current year.
Sandwell	With limited funding opportunities, strategy gets steered towards available funding.
Sefton	In theory we could link to the Internet now, but costs and staff shortage preclude it at present and I cannot speculate as to when it will come to pass.
Somerset	We play a key role in the management of the county council's Website and intranet.
Staffordshire	IT strategy built into library plan. Success of developments dependent on successful implementation of network and commitment of staff to adapt to changes and availability of finance to support initiatives.
Stockton	Stockton borough libraries became an independent library authority in April 1996, having previously been Cleveland county council. Fortunately the council has invested in libraries in the first year by finding funding for our new computer system. We are all very excited having gone LIVE in every branch in April 1997. As you can imagine lots of things are in the pipeline. We look forward to your 1998 questionnaire when hopefully we will be able to answer yes to everything!
Upper Norwood	We hope to have Heritage installed soon! However, further developments are likely to happen later rather than sooner given the speed that suppliers work.
West Sussex	The library service has been charged with developing, in collaboration with the head of the information systems and technology strategy, a corporate information strategy for the authority.
Western Isles	Is it just part of the myth or are we really so far behind?
Wigan	All libraries have access to a list-type union catalogue for the Authority. Data for the 3 libraries using BookshelF is downloaded from this. Union Catalogue is on council mainframe which also runs acquisitions and financial management system.

Authority	Comments
Wrexham	As a relatively new and very small county we are starting from a low IT base. We are currently installing the Galaxy 2000 system which we hope eventually to have in use at all 12 libraries in the county. OPAC facilities will be available at the central library from January. Internet access is being developed, and networking systems possibly linking to the county borough's own developments are being considered.

Information technology in public libraries 1997: the questionnaire

3. ONLINE SEARCHING, OTHER THAN INTERNET	
IF YOU UNDERTAKE ONLINE SEARCHING, LIST THE MOST POPULAR DATABASES?	

4. PUBLIC ACCESS PCS	
4.1 In how many libraries do you provide PCs for open learning?	
4.2 How many PCs in total provided for open learning?	
4.3 In how many libraries do you provide PCs for hire?	
4.4 How many PCs in total provided for hire?	
4.5 Do you offer user training schemes for these services	YES NO

5. INTERNET	
5.1 Does your library service have access to the internet?	YES NO
5.2 How many PCs in your library authority have internet access	
5.3 How many of the total are for public access	
5.4 How many libraries in your authority have internet access	
5.5 How many of these service points offer public access?	
TO ACHIEVE ACCESS HOW MANY OF THESE SERVICE POINTS USE	
5.6 Leased lines	
5.7 Dial-up	
5.8 Council network	
WHICH MEMBERS OF STAFF HAVE INTERNET ACCESS	
5.9 Technical	
5.10 Senior Management	
5.11 Reference Staff	
5.12 Other	
HOW IS THE INTERNET USED BY STAFF?	

5.13 Reference work	
5.14 Professional awareness	
5.15 Communication (e.g. email)	
5.16 Exploration/experimentation	
5.17 Online databases	
5.18 Systems support	
5.19 Cataloguing and acquisitions	
5.20 Other (please specify):	

6. CHARGING POLICIES

PLEASE (INDICATE CHARGES AND POLICIES FOR THE FOLLOWING)

6.1 CD Rom	
6.2 Online searching	
6.3 Public access to pcs	
6.4 Open for learning	
6.5 Internet	

7. COMMUNITY INFORMATION	
HOW HAVE YOU AUTOMATED YOURCOMMUNITY INFORMATION SYSTEM?	
7.1 Library management system	
7.2 Teletext	
7.4 PC with a database management system	
7.5 Wordprocessor	
7.6 Internet	
HOW IS THE INFORMATION MADE AVAILABLE?	
7.7 Online to staff	
7.8 Online to public	
7.9 Printed copies	

8. ELECTRONIC PUBLIC INFORMATION POINTS	
IF YOU ARE INVOLVED WITH THE MANAGEMENT OF KIOSKS, ETC.	
8.1 Which software system is used?	
8.2 How many access points are there within your authority?	
8.3 How many of those points are Internet compatible?	
8.4 If you provide Internet access to your information, please provide the URL	

9. TELECENTRES

DO YOU HAVE PLANS OR DO YOU HAVE ALREADY TELECENTRES SUCH AS INPUT/OUTPUT, CYBERIA, ETC. IN ANY OF YOUR LIBRARIES? (PLEASE GIVE DETAILS OF THE SERVICES PROVIDED, AVAILABILITY AND ANY PARTNERSHIPS)

10. MANAGEMENT AND STAFF TRAINING

PLEASE DESCRIBE ARRANGEMENTS FOR THE TECHNICAL MANAGEMENT OF SYSTEMS, EG SPECIALIST STAFF, ETC AND ANY ARRANGEMENTS FOR STAFF TRAINING AND AWARENESS

11. FUTURE PLANS

FUTURE PLANS - PLEASE DESCRIBE ANY CONCRETE PLANS FOR IT DEVELOPMENTS WHICH YOU THINK IT WILL BE POSSIBLE TO IMPLEMENT BY THE END OF 1997/98

12. IT STRATEGIES

Do you have a written down it strategy for your service?	YES NO

IF THE ANSWER TO THIS QUESTION IS YES, IT WOULD BE EXTREMELY HELPFUL IF YOU COULD ENCLOSE A COPY WITH THIS QUESTIONNAIRE. THE CONTENT WILL NOT BE ATTRIBUTED TO YOU WITHOUT YOUR AGREEMENT

AND FINALLY...

ARE THERE ANY OTHER COMMENTS YOU WOULD LIKE TO MAKE?

PLEASE RETURN THE COMPLETED QUESTIONNAIRE BY 1 JUNE 1997 TO:

Chris Batt
Croydon Clocktower
Katharine Street
Croydon CR9 IET
TEL: 0181 253 1000
FAX: 0181 253 1004
EMAIL: lbcbatt@croydon.gov.uk